From the Institute of Policy Studies'
Singapore Perspectives

Insights on Singapore's Politics and Governance from Leading Thinkers

From the Institute of Policy Studies'
Singapore Perspectives

Insights on Singapore's Politics and Governance from Leading Thinkers

Institute of Policy Studies, Singapore

Lee Kuan Yew
School of Public Policy
National University of Singapore

iPS Institute of
Policy Studies

World Scientific

Published by

World Scientific Publishing Co. Pte. Ltd.

5 Toh Tuck Link, Singapore 596224

USA office: 27 Warren Street, Suite 401-402, Hackensack, NJ 07601

UK office: 57 Shelton Street, Covent Garden, London WC2H 9HE

British Library Cataloguing-in-Publication Data
A catalogue record for this book is available from the British Library.

INSIGHTS ON SINGAPORE'S POLITICS AND GOVERNANCE FROM
LEADING THINKERS
From the Institute of Policy Studies' Singapore Perspectives

ISBN 978-981-120-484-5
ISBN 978-981-120-502-6 (pbk)

For any available supplementary material, please visit
https://www.worldscientific.com/worldscibooks/10.1142/11401#t=suppl

Desk Editor: Jiang Yulin

Contents

Contents

CHAPTER 1

Singapore's Emerging Informal Public Sphere

CHERIAN GEORGE

INTRODUCTION

One of the major media milestones that Singapore crossed in 2006 was the introduction of High Definition TV or HDTV. Offering extremely high resolution widescreen pictures coupled with the benefits of digital interactivity and more channels, HDTV was showed off at selected public places such as community clubs. The Media Development Authority and private-sector technology partners were banking on the likelihood that crystal clear images of glistening dew on the tip of a leaf in a nature documentary, or the instantly spottable golf ball sent zipping through the air by Tiger Woods, would convince Singaporeans to embrace HDTV and justify the investments in this new technology.

Ironically, however, the televisual trend that caught on in 2006 without any formal encouragement had a screen size of about one-fortieth of a HDTV set, and grainy pictures reminiscent of the work of an impressionist painter not wearing his glasses. This was of course YouTube, which became the flagship of the movement known as user-generated content — a movement supposedly so significant that *Time* magazine named You as its Person of the Year. Together with blogs and other communication technologies, YouTube is helping to turn "the journalism of the lecture" into "the journalism of the conversation" (Gillmor, 2004).

One key question is what impact this development has for the public sphere — the space where citizens discuss and deliberate matters of common interest and public concern, and hold the state accountable. It is tempting to frame the trend in competitive terms, as a battle between traditional mainstream media and alternative new media for supremacy in the public sphere. However, although there are some competitive aspects to this dynamic, it is useful to view it also as a complementary relationship, just as "Off-Off-Broadway" productions are part of the same ecology that also produces high-end Broadway hits, and garage tinkering is organically tied to high-end research laboratories. Social theorists suggest that the public sphere isn't and shouldn't be unitary or monolithic. We should instead think in terms of a *formal* public sphere that is complemented by multiple *informal* public spheres. The formal public sphere is where the broadest national issues are discussed, consensus is sought, and negotiation and social conciliation is practised. It's where people figure out their common interests and work through their shared problems as a Public. This is the role that national newspapers and broadcast channels are well suited for.[1] Indeed, to the extent that nations are imagined communities (Anderson, 1991), the national media are principal "imagineers", to borrow a job title from the Disney corporation.

However, the norms and protocols that are necessary for the proper functioning of the formal public sphere typically exclude and marginalise minority points of view, even in the freest of liberal societies. Therefore, the informal public sphere plays an important role in allowing broad participation; they are the spaces where people can share ideas more freely. "Here," says Jürgen Habermas (1996), "new problem situations can be perceived more sensitively, discourses aimed at achieving self-understanding can be conducted more widely and expressively, collective identities and need interpretations can be articulated with fewer compulsions than is the case in procedurally regulated [formal] public spheres." These are the roles that user-generated alternative media, with their low barriers to entry, are exceedingly well suited to.

An informal public sphere is not new either as an idea or as a social phenomenon. In Singapore, however, it may take some getting used to. People's Action Party (PAP) ideology has emphasised consensus rather than the expression of dissonant viewpoints. This ideology has been institutionalised in the media system, with strict licensing laws ensuring that the mainstream media are under the duopoly control of large, trusted corporations. The proliferation of niche and alternative media has put pressure on mainstream media and on the government.

CHALLENGES FOR MAINSTREAM MEDIA

Singapore's mainstream media are being challenged on a number of fronts — profits, readership and viewership, and influence. Blogs and other user-generated content are only part of that challenge, and indeed the mainstream media were in gradual decline long before blogging. The audience's attention is dissipating across a wider diversity of media forms. At the same time, the advertisers that used to reward newspapers for their ability to congregate the masses now have alternative outlets, ranging from niche magazines to public transport vehicles.

This decline needs to be put in perspective: newspapers are still the most profitable media businesses, and still occupy the commanding heights of the news business; it is just that its degree of dominance is slipping.[2] Mainstream media's superior resources should mean that they will continue to be able to offer more and better content than most of their competitors. However, as general interest media, the mainstream media cannot hope to serve all of the people all of the time. As Singapore society becomes increasingly complex and variegated, as sub-cultures proliferate, and as tastes become increasingly specialised, it is getting tougher for the national media to serve all of the people even *some* of the time.

Media companies around the world are responding by spinning off more niche publications and supplements. There are two problems with this approach. One is that not all readers are created equal in media companies' eyes. If you have the disposable income to shop for cars, luxury watches, designer clothes and spa vacations, media companies will pander to you in order to deliver you to their advertisers. Readers of lesser means are less attractive to advertisers and are thus unlikely to see the creation of magazines, supplements or special sections on such themes as how to reduce household bills or maintain emotional health through methods other than shopping. In a country with a growing and already sizeable socio-economic divide, there is a risk of large segments being unserved by the media. There is another problem with going niche. While people want to nurture their own unique identities and pursue their own interests and lifestyles, society as a whole would be poorer if there were no common spaces left. If the national media appealed to all of the people *none* of the time, one would have to ask if there is anything Singaporean about Singapore any more. Therefore, the mainstream media need to balance individual desires for niche content with the social need for common spaces. This is easier said than done, but must remain a top priority.

Space for Alternative Views

Another challenge faced by mainstream media is their handicap in reflecting alternative views. This is the result of two distinct attributes. The most obvious is the burden of operating under a government licence. The regulatory regime requires mainstream media not to try to set the political agenda, which in practice means that editors are expected to filter out or at least not over-amplify views that contradict government positions on key principles or policies. Alternative media on the Internet are not subject to discretionary licensing and therefore enjoy much wider latitude in expressing contrary views (George, 2006).

In addition to political constraints in countries such as Singapore, the mainstream media around the world also operate with a technical disadvantage. Paradoxically, the professional operations and high production values associated with mainstream media seem to be creating a counter-demand for a more personal, supposedly authentic experience via cottage-industry media. This phenomenon is not unique to the news media industry: it seems to apply to most cultural and lifestyle products (Carroll and Hannan, 2000). Thus, there are beer connoisseurs who would shun Tiger and Heineken and opt for microbrews and homebrews, despite the latter's inconsistent quality. Similarly, music lovers may scoff at assembly-line boy bands, no matter how slick, and seek out underground, garage bands. This tendency may also explain the aforementioned appeal of YouTube, despite the seemingly superior quality control exercised by the TV industry. The imperfect but personally crafted and authentic is being embraced as an antidote to the impersonal and industrial, no matter how professional the latter.

Can Singapore's mainstream media overcome this twin handicap of licensing and industrial standards? The dichotomous regulatory regime — with stricter supervision of mainstream media and more latitude for niche and/or alternative media — is likely to be preserved. However, since think tanks are supposed to think the unthinkable, I would be shortchanging this IPS forum if I failed to at least raise the question of reviewing the Newspaper and Printing Presses Act. It is noteworthy that in Malaysia, which has a comparable newspaper permit system, the Malaysian Human Rights Commission has called for the following amendments: making permits permanent rather than requiring annual renewal; making the granting of permits automatic, subject to objections from security agencies; and requiring the government to publish reasons for permit rejection, which can then be challenged in court (Suhakam, 2003).

Liberalising licensing rules (and aggressively upholding competition laws) could have the positive effect of diversifying the regulated mainstream segment of Singapore's media. Media entrepreneurs and professionals would have the freedom to explore new business models and editorial concepts. While these are unlikely to displace *The Straits Times* as the country's number one daily, they could offer the public options that do not currently exist. In other sectors such as education and healthcare, industry restructuring over the past decade has allowed the emergence of more providers and allowed them greater autonomy, thus multiplying choice for Singaporeans. Regulators of local news media are relative laggards in this regard.

Realistically speaking, Singapore is unlikely to engage the question of licensing any time in the near future; it may be more practical to consider less out-of-the-box options. Even if the letter of the law is not revised, the government needs to adapt to a changing environment and calibrate its controls accordingly. In supervising the mainstream media, regulators and internal gatekeepers should avoid widening the gap between mainstream and alternative media. I hesitate to call it a *credibility* gap, because most people do believe that the mainstream media are by and large accurate and believable. For reasons I have touched on earlier, it should perhaps be called an *authenticity* gap — the mainstream media are seen as somehow failing to provide an authentic experience; to be presenting the news accurately, yes, but not *for* you and me — unlike, say, a favourite blog.

Mainstream media can try to respond by providing more space for user-generated content and a sampling of that other world, which is precisely what *The Straits Times* is trying to do through STOMP and what *Today* tried to do by enlisting the blogger, mr brown, as a columnist. The failure of that experiment and its backfiring on *Today*'s reputation showed how dicey this challenge is. Responding to one of mr brown's *Today* columns, the government said that while mr brown was entitled to his views, "opinions which are widely circulated in a regular column in a serious newspaper should meet higher standards" (Bhavani, 2006). It added, "If a columnist presents himself as a non-political observer, while exploiting his access to the mass media to undermine the Government's standing with the electorate, then he is no longer a constructive critic, but a partisan player in politics."

Bridging the Divide

It is unclear whether *Today*'s immediate termination of mr brown's column was instigated by the government. Undoubtedly, though, the authorities believed that the particular offending article should not have been published in that form. Mainstream media editors have thus been sternly reminded not to abdicate their responsibility, as gatekeepers of the formal public sphere, to filter the strident voices and other noise of the hoi polloi. For the mainstream media's own good as well as for Singapore's, however, we should avoid erecting a firewall between mainstream and alternative media. Ideas need to flow between the two. The national media should have the latitude to reflect the buzz of alternative spaces. But, after the government's statements in 2006, can they? The sternness of their warning notwithstanding, the authorities may not be totally opposed to newspapers reporting or republishing online viewpoints as long as three criteria are met. First, of course, the statements quoted must not cross any boundaries of law or good taste. Second, avant-garde or minority views should not be misrepresented as reflecting mainstream or majority views. Third, the mainstream media should be mindful of the power they possess to bequeath symbolic status on the people and perspectives they give space to, and should therefore be judicious in whether and how they do so.

These may seem onerous rules, but they are not impossible to work with. Existing journalistic conventions allow newspapers to carry diverse content by applying a range of editing standards, which are signalled clearly to the reader. For example, regular readers know that the views that *The Straits Times* regards as most authoritative are to be found in its own editorial and in columns such as "Thinking Aloud". At the other extreme are its user-generated content pages — and even among these there is a clear hierarchy, with the "Forum" page at the top and other sections for reader contributions — including online views — given lower status. Similarly, clear signalling tells the reader that the "YouthInk" is not to be treated as seriously as more grown-up columns. The issue is not so much that readers are likely to get confused, but that editors require deniability: for their own protection, in a tightly regulated environment, they need to be able to distance themselves from content that they carry for the sake of providing a comprehensive range of viewpoints. In hindsight, perhaps *Today*'s mistake was to give mr brown's column the same look and feel of its more elevated columns, thus apparently giving the editors' stamp of approval to the arguments therein. *Today*'s relatively small staff of full-time writers creates a greater reliance on user-generated content; these and even humour columns are not distinguished particularly clearly from more considered viewpoints. To borrow the words of Singapore's eloquent former information minister George Yeo, *Today*'s design was and continues to be a case of *boh tua boh suay*.[3]

All in all, mainstream media editors can probably be trusted to preserve the distinction between formal and informal public spheres, and not to go overboard with user-generated content. After all, it would be self-defeating to do so, compromising their main competitive advantage in professionally produced content. However, there is a real risk that certain other professional standards will be compromised due to the competitive pressure posed by alternative media. Digital delivery and fewer layers of checks sometimes enable alternative media to be the first with the news. Professional journalists know that they are supposed to "get it first but first get it right". Unfortunately, once the alternative media release a piece of news, there is pressure on mainstream media to publish it on the grounds that it is already "out there". There is plenty of evidence worldwide to suggest that this risk is already materialising, short-circuiting the standard, rigorous checks that journalists know they are supposed to exercise (Kovach and Rosenstiel, 1999). Usually, newspapers will try to hide their less scrupulous judgments with a fig leaf, suggesting that although the gossip they are recirculating has not been verified, the fact that is creating a buzz is eminently newsworthy and reportable. Singapore's national newspaper is not immune to such tendencies: the front page of *The Sunday Times* was recently splashed with sexy photos of a model that, according to online speculation, was the Mongolian woman who had been murdered in Malaysia. It turned out that she was a Korean model unconnected with the sordid affair.

In appealing to the mainstream media not to imitate the alternative media in some respects, I do not want to give the impression that the national newspapers and broadcasters are always the paragons of virtue and guardians of high standards, while the alternative media are irresponsible and anti-national. On the contrary, with mainstream media becoming increasingly commercial in its impulses, the informal public sphere is seen by many Singaporeans as the more hospitable space for contributing to public life. Indeed, one could say that there is at least as much nation-building going on in the alternative media as there is in the national mainstream media. Of course, if you define nation-building in old-fashioned top-down terms — equating it merely with treating the nation's leaders with deference and amplifying their messages — then the mainstream media have the edge. However, if we adopt the contemporary understanding of nation-building as a bottom-up process of active citizenship, *à la* Singapore 21 and Remaking Singapore, then the action is increasingly in the alternative media. In a growing number of sectors — heritage and history, the arts, natural history and the environment, local music and culture, even the National Service experience — the most passionate and knowledgeable efforts to connect Singaporeans with their nation are taking place in the informal public sphere.

Increasingly, the national media are adopting commercial marketability rather than nation-building as their touchstone. They are getting away with it partly because they are careful to continue playing their traditional top-down nation-building role and thus appease their political masters. Besides, they are business entities, it's their money, and it's their prerogative to make investment decisions. On the other hand, Singapore's media giants are protected by government licensing. As custodians of scarce, publicly granted publishing and broadcasting permits, they owe a fiduciary responsibility to the public. Furthermore, if the news media choose to be ever more entertainment-driven, consumer-driven and accommodating to advertisers, then the traditional professional values of journalism as a public service will be increasingly marginalised. This is a worldwide trend, prompting the *Economist* (2006) to speculate that the mission of high-quality journalism will have to find a new home, migrating from newspapers to other types of organisation, such as NGOs and citizen groups.

CHALLENGES FOR GOVERNMENT

Singapore's emerging informal public sphere poses special challenges for a government accustomed to dealing with the public through the more pliable and predictable national media. One valid concern is whether public communication during national crises will be compromised by rumour and disinformation through alternative media. This risk may be overblown. Particularly during emergencies, people seek reliable and credible sources. As long as the government's public communication is prompt, comprehensive, transparent, and receives full mainstream media support, false information will gain no foothold. For example, public communication during the Sars epidemic and after the Jemaah Islamiyah (JI) arrests was widely viewed as a success, despite the existence of unregulated Internet media. It is when there is a lack of reliable information that rumour will fill the vacuum. If the government learns from positive examples such as its management of Sars and the Jemaah Islamiyah (JI) affair, there is little reason to fear the blogosphere during emergencies.

Aside from emergencies, it is certainly the case that government efforts to explain its policies must now contend with a counter-discourse from alternative media. The record so far would have probably convinced the government that much of this counter-discourse is of low quality and not particularly productive. On the other hand, the government appears to have correctly assessed that it is neither possible nor necessary to extend its "nail every lie" approach into the alternative online space. The noise on the blogosphere may be irritating to policy-makers but there is little evidence that it has corrupted the public mind or compromised the quality of governance. In most policy areas, the critical question is not how much noise surrounds the public, but how the public ultimately acts at the point of decision. Arguably, the public has shown itself to be capable and willing to act on sound information rather than over-react to every unreliable morsel that they come across online or in coffeeshop talk.

Probably the hardest development for the government to get used to will be the idea that it can no longer monopolise the shaping of the broad public agenda and the managing of its own reputation and status. We are witnessing a democratisation of influence. In the alternative media, reputation matters but rank and status *per se* are not respected. In engaging online discourse, the government cannot "pull rank". Arguments will be won or lost on their merits.

I have tried to argue here that alternative media have contributed to a reconstitution of the public sphere in Singapore. In addition to the formal public sphere — where national-level policy debates take place and where the public decides on its common future — there is a growing informal public sphere, with lower barriers to entry admitting a greater diversity of views and with a greater tolerance for inadequately processed information. Most of the discussion in the mainstream media, dominated by politicians and mainstream commentators, has predictably focused on the negative implications of this widening informal public sphere. However, there are a number of possible positive outcomes. First, wider and more intense deliberation can lead to more sensitive and nuanced policy-making. This is not automatic, but would depend on the aggregation, organisation and translation of myriad points of view into forms that can be acted on. Such mediation can be done by individuals and groups within government or the mainstream media or the people sector — and preferably all of them. Second, unruly communication in the informal public sphere may seem unconstructive, but public servants need greater exposure to such unregulated interventions if only for their professional development. The requisite skills for dealing with such challenges may have been irrelevant for technocratic "head versus heart" decision-making, but they are increasingly important for a new kind of politics in which intangibles such as values, culture and identity have come to the fore. Third, the informal public sphere has a nation-building function. This is not only because active participants feel a greater sense of ownership in the nation, but also because of the positive externalities that voluntary participation generates. The small communities of common interest that are coalescing around blogs and other alternative media can be building blocks for nation-building.

The communication that takes place in the informal public sphere has many obvious flaws. A lot of what circulates is silly and irrelevant at best, and at worst, tasteless, mean, small-hearted, intolerant and stupid. One hopes that 2007 and the coming years will see a certain maturing of the alternative media. This, however, would pose an intriguing dilemma for the establishment. As things stand, the superior quality of the mainstream national media benefits established political and business interests: the media are used as a vehicle of influence by the government, and as a wellspring of profit by big business. The media of the informal public sphere are not so easily harnessed. This matters little at present, because of the quality divide between mainstream and alternative media. However, if the divide were to disappear, the alternative media would generate its own quality dividend — which would not automatically accrue to the political and commercial powers that be, but would instead be up for grabs by new players. While Singapore's political and media elite routinely rail against the inferiority of blogs and other informal media, there is only one thing worse for the elite: alternative media that actually do improve in quality, reach and influence.

ENDNOTES

1. Whether the mainstream media actually do fulfil the role of the public sphere is debatable. Habermas, who is most associated with this idea, observed that the media are dominated by powerful political and economic interests that subvert their potential as agents of the public sphere.

2. Singapore Press Holdings' core operations showed net earnings of $361.1 million for the year ended 31 August 2006. In line with an improving economy, this represented 2.6 per cent growth over the previous year.

3. In Hokkein, literally means "no big, no small".

REFERENCES

Anderson, B. *Imagined Communities: Reflections on the Origins and Spread of Nationalism.* Verso, London, 1991.

Bhavani, K. "Distorting the Truth, mr brown?" *Today*, 3 July 2006.

Carroll, G. and Hannan M. *The Demography of Corporations and Industries.* Princeton University Press, Princeton, New Jersey, 2000.

Economist. "Who Killed the Newspaper?" 24 August 2006.

George, C. *Contentious Journalism: Towards Democratic Discourse in Malaysia and Singapore.* Singapore University Press, Singapore, and University of Washington Press, Seattle, Washington, 2006.

Gillmor, D. *We the Media.* O'Reilly Media, Sebastopol, CA, 2004.

Habermas, J. *Between Facts and Norms.* MIT Press, Cambridge, MA, 1996.

Kovach, B. and Rosenstiel T. *Warp Speed: America in the Age of Mixed Media.* Century Foundation, New York, 1999.

Suhakam. *A Case for Media Freedom: Report of Suhakam's Workshop on Freedom of the Media.* Human Rights Commission of Malaysia, Kuala Lumpur, Malaysia, 2003. Available online at http://www.suhakam.org.my.

CHAPTER 2

Forging New Paths with Audacity and Vision

PETER ONG

In this talk, I will provide you with my best visualisation of Singapore now and in the years to come, and my thoughts on the issues which are at the heart of the matter.

NEW PARADIGM NEEDED: FOLLOWING FOOTSTEPS TO FORGING PATHS

First off, I will discuss where Singapore is today. From 1965 to 2009, Singapore underwent a remarkable transformation, from the initial steps of nation building to our push to be a "Global City of Distinction" and the "Best Home for All". We have done very well. The smarts, dedication and hard work of our political and public service leaders and the aligned and joint efforts of our business enterprises and citizens have all helped Singapore achieve much success in this short period. Although geographically Singapore is and always will be a little red dot, we have punched above our weight. Nowadays, Singapore is considered a "giant" in the world economy. Talented people of all nationalities are flocking here and we have evolved into a cosmopolitan city of world-class standards. Recent events bear strong testimony to Singapore's place in the world: it was to Temasek Holdings and the Government of Singapore Investment Corporation (GIC) that world-class companies came a-calling for assistance during the present financial crisis.

As we move towards 2015, when we will be (gasp) half a century old, there will be fewer footsteps of great countries and cities for us to follow, and there will be fewer blueprints of success that we can rely on, to "rapidly copy and smartly improve upon". Moving forward, Singapore can no longer afford to "follow the footsteps of others". Rather, we must embrace new ways of thinking and seeing the world, and bravely and confidently forge new paths ahead. This is one of the roles and responsibilities of well-respected, well-regarded First World countries, and we in Singapore must play our part. We must forge new paths at a strong clip to catch up with established cities like New York, London, and San Francisco; and we must ensure that we stay (way) ahead of rapidly emerging cities in Asia like Shanghai, Beijing, Mumbai and Bangalore. Other than competing on a city-by-city basis, retaining our position of strength amongst the other Asian Tiger economies of Hong Kong, Taiwan and South Korea remains part of the game.

Forty-four years post-independence, Singapore is at the forefront of the First World. By many established yardsticks of success, we have indeed arrived. The questions we need to ask today: "How can we sustain our success?" and "How can we get better?"

NEW FLYING INSTRUMENTS REQUIRED:
THE X-RAY AND THE MRI

Albert Einstein once said: "We cannot solve problems by using the same kind of thinking we used when we created them." Singapore is exactly at this juncture. To forge new paths, we need new tools, new dashboards, new visualisations, new methods, improved insights, and an enhanced way of alignment and collaboration across government ministries, statutory boards, associated agencies, private enterprises, citizens and Permanent Residents. Just as the scanning by MRI (magnetic resonance imaging) was a vast improvement over the X-ray in the field of medical imaging, and that both of them are very much needed in healthcare today, we need to keep the best of the old and complement that with the new and improved. Over the next few minutes, I will share with you some frameworks and visualisations which I believe will be helpful in facilitating Singapore to further improve and achieve.

First off, let us talk about the power of leading indicators. Leading indicators are metrics that allow policy makers and business leaders to anticipate and predict the future, and thereafter to take smart moves and wise steps to create the most positive and meaningful future possible. Here is an interesting story on leading indicators. In May 2007, when Gallup Chairman & CEO Jim Clifton and I were preparing for a series of senior political leader meetings in Singapore, we looked at data and patterns from the United States. And one of the interesting things we saw, from Gallup's Daily Poll in America, was that Americans were saying that they did not have as much "spare change" as they would like to get on with their lives, to spend it on things which they enjoy and which bring them happiness. Also, the number of Americans who said that they worried about money, that they sometimes struggled to put food on the table and a shelter above their families' heads, was increasing. These patterns and insights surprised Jim and I as America appeared to be doing rather well at that time. We then looked at data across large American companies. And we were struck by what we saw was happening at huge companies like Wal-Mart. Wal-Mart was cancelling and postponing large orders from low-cost countries like China. What was happening?

When Jim and I met up with the senior political leaders in Singapore in June 2007, we openly shared the insights and visualisations that we saw, and admitted that we did not have all the answers. But we told them that the writing was on the wall. Something rather large and very bad is looming in the distance in America, the economy was starting to slow rather dramatically and that people on Main Street and companies on Wall Street were seeing and feeling it, and the growing problem was being reflected in the behaviours, feelings, thoughts and actions of Americans and American corporations as captured by Gallup's Daily Poll in America. Fast forward to today. We all know what happened next. Wall Street, the sub-prime crisis, and the economy of America tanked... ... and took the whole world along with it. We are in the midst of this global downturn, and people all across the world, including many Singaporeans, are hurting. Wal-Mart postponing and cancelling large orders: that is a leading indicator of the extent of the downturn. Greater numbers of Americans not having "spare change", or the personal economics to get around, struggling to put food on the table and a roof over their family's heads, these are also leading indicators.

Leading indicators are essential and necessary to anticipate and predict the future way in advance such that the right steps can be taken, early and proactively. Leveraged well, leading indicators will allow us to see in the horizon, all sorts of swans, white or black.

Forging new paths as we move forward rather than simply following footsteps will necessitate that Singapore's leaders jointly gaze at a crystal ball of leading indicators, such that multiple ministries, statutory boards and agencies can all take aligned and oftentimes complex steps and actions way in advance to influence Singapore and Singaporeans, such that a better future can be created. Doing so will allow Singapore to navigate the waters ahead as best as we can. Leading indicators strategically and smartly analysed will facilitate sense-making, decision-making, policy-making and the most important of all, future-making. Leading indicators will allow Singapore and Singaporeans to forge new paths ahead, especially when the vista is not all that clear.

Table 1 Singapore ranks highly on a number of indices, and not so highly on others

How Singapore Stands

Where Singapore is Top	Singapore's Score
Law & Order Index	97
National institutions Index	87
Youth Development Index	92
Food & Shelter Index	98
Community Basics Index	91
Personal Health Index	90

Where Singapore Needs Improvement	Singapore's Score
Work Index	44
Personal Economics Index	67
Positive Experience Index	64
Thriving Index	49
Diversity Index	61
Optimism Index	62

Gallup surveys 140 countries every year on 100 core questions. We know what 98 percent of the world's population is thinking, feeling, and what their opinions, pain and happy points are. Singapore stands at the absolute top, whether compared as a country or as a city, on six of Gallup's indices (See Table 1):

- Law & Order
- National Institutions
- Youth Development
- Food & Shelter
- Community Basics
- Personal Health

These are areas where Singapore's value proposition is at its strongest. Many of them are the reasons that businesses and talents relocate their headquarters here and why citizens and PRs are so satisfied with Singapore as a place to live, work and play. Satisfaction for a country or city can often be attained through strong national, financial and community infrastructure, especially when there is an absence in its citizens and PRs of negative feelings like sadness, pain, suffering and depression. Singapore excels in these areas. On the other hand, engagement for a country or city necessitates the presence of positive feelings like optimism, hope, efficacy, laughter, a full arrestment of the senses, *et cetera*, in addition to the absence of negative feelings. This is where Singapore needs to improve. Helping Singaporeans find a job which they enjoy and which best utilises their talents other than just finding a job *per se*, increasing their hope and optimism levels and the number of positive experiences they encounter, inculcating the belief that they are thriving rather than just surviving, *et cetera*, these are areas which I believe Singapore seriously needs to focus on, so as to propel itself to the forefront of the First World. If we can nail these areas where we are already in the top one-third of all countries polled by Gallup, Singapore will be second to none, where businesses and talents, foreign or home-grown, will find most engaging to live, work, play, and more importantly, achieve.

BUSINESS CONCEPTS EXTENDED: POPULATION SEGMENTS, ENGAGED CITIZENS AND CRM

In business speak, we talk about "Customer Segments", "Engaged Customers" and "CRM", or Customer Relationship Management. Many a Chairman, CEO and CFO knows and believes strongly that customers are the lifeblood of any organisation, and that the more the enterprise does to strongly engage and retain them, the better their business, revenue and profits will be. If we are to extend these very important and very useful business concepts to Singapore, we will be able to better improve and impact the lives of Singaporeans. Let me explain what I mean. Other than simply thinking about Singapore as a country or a city, we can think of Singapore in terms of "Population Segments" very much like "Customer Segments", "Engaged Citizens" very much like "Engaged Customers" and "Citizen Relationship Management" rather than "Customer Relationship Management". Think about how powerful such a visualisation will be. If our policy makers, political and public sector leaders are to leverage these new concepts and see Singapore as made up of various citizen segments, all waiting, wanting and needing to be tightly engaged, and embrace and embark on Citizen Relationship Management initiatives, we will all be able to move one step closer to building engaged Singaporeans whose hearts, minds, thoughts and actions are all for, and about Singapore.

Chart 1 Citizen engagement is built on several components, with each component being represented by one to two statements

Citizen Engagement

Increased Community, City and Country Commitment & Effectiveness

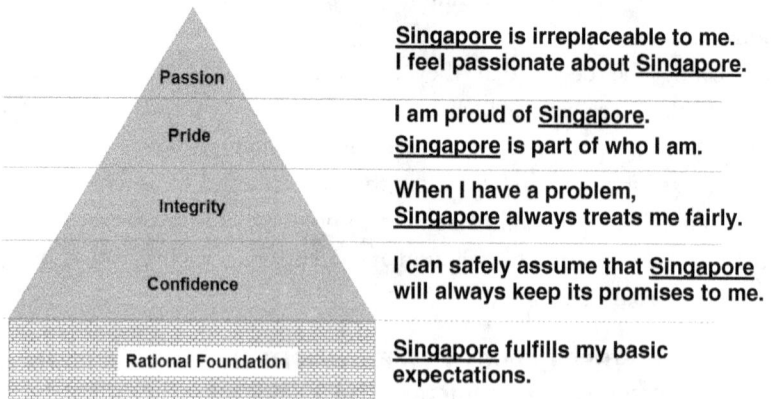

Passion	Singapore is irreplaceable to me. I feel passionate about Singapore.
Pride	I am proud of Singapore. Singapore is part of who I am.
Integrity	When I have a problem, Singapore always treats me fairly.
Confidence	I can safely assume that Singapore will always keep its promises to me.
Rational Foundation	Singapore fulfills my basic expectations.

As Singapore is already operating in the First World, many of our citizens' basic expectations of what a country and a city should provide have already been met. What does this mean? This means that in the Citizen Engagement hierarchy, both the Confidence and Integrity components as well as the Rational Foundation component are well-met and well-achieved (See Chart 1). It is in the higher-order areas of Pride and Passion where Singapore's leaders need to turbocharge improvement. We need to come up with new ideas and implement new steps to create, build and sustain the Pride and Passion of Singaporeans about Singapore. We need Singaporeans to say the following:

- I am proud of Singapore.
- Singapore is part of who I am.
- Singapore is irreplaceable to me.
- I feel passionate about Singapore.

The more Singaporeans and PRs are able to say these, the higher the level of Engaged Citizenry in Singapore, and the greater the commitment and effectiveness of our communities to our city. I am convinced that Engaged Citizenry is one of the most important key performance indicators which a country's leaders can strive for and attain, be it in Singapore or otherwise.

What have we covered so far? One, moving forward, we need to forge new paths rather than to follow footsteps. Two, to do so, we need new flying instruments. Like the X-ray and the MRI, we need both tactical, process-based measures and we need strategic, behavioural-based ones. We need a mix of leading and lagging indicators. Three, we need new concepts. Population segments to think about our citizens and PRs, Engaged Citizens as a target to strive and shoot for, and Citizen Relationship Management or CRM as a new discipline that will enable Singapore to strategically and systematically build and attain Engaged Citizenry. What else do we need, for Singapore to be a Global City of Distinction and to be the Best Home for All?

GLOBAL CITY OF DISTINCTION AND BEST HOME FOR ALL: DIFFERENT STROKES FOR DIFFERENT FOLKS

Basically, we need different strokes for different folks. Just like every customer segment needs to be differently targeted, marketed and catered to, so do different population segments. In June last year, *The Business Times* published an article I wrote, titled "Take a good look at the 'Soul of the City'".

The article talked about how city planners and policy makers in cities and communities need to take a serious look at behavioural economic concepts and approaches and put them into practice, such that the cities and communities which they lead will become better places to live, work and play.

In a nutshell, the Soul of a City is determined by the collective experiences and responses of its citizens to three sub-indices relating to Engaged Citizenry, Emotional Well-Being and Personal Expression. The higher the Soul score, the more endearing a city to its residents, the greater the likelihood that residents will flourish in the city, achieve their dreams and contribute strongly to the city's achievements and outputs. Soul, an "outcome" measure, can be proactively impacted by what one calls "driver" measures. An "outcome" measure, by the way, is a measure or score (usually quantitative) that reflects the overall assessment of a product, service or situation on an overall basis, after taking everything into consideration. "Outcome" measures could reflect a state of being (e.g., overall satisfaction with life in Singapore) or be an indicator of likely behaviour in the future (such as the willingness to recommend Singapore as a great place to settle in). "Driver" measures on the other hand are factors that impact the "outcome measure". Most times multiple drivers impact the "outcome" measure, each usually having a differing extent of impact; "Driver measures may differ from time to time, depending on the circumstances surrounding the moment and depending on the population segments one is performing the analysis on".

A talk on Soul will take a full hour by itself. As we do not have the luxury of time today, let me quickly provide you a simple analysis of what the primary drivers of Soul are for some population segments in Singapore, as measured by our survey of 1,500 nationally-representative, randomly-sampled Singaporeans in August 2008. Jobs. Jobs. Jobs. At this very moment, employment is the most important driver for Soul for most population segments in Singapore (See Table 2). For other population segments, like the 40–59 age group, it is Community Basics in the form of Social Infrastructure, like the availability of quality healthcare and affordable housing. For the 60s and above age group, it is Prosperity which

20

Table 2 Employment is the top concern for most Singaporeans across the board

Different Strokes for Different Folks

By Education Levels	Primary Driver for Soul
University	Jobs
Polytechnic	Jobs
O & A Levels, ITE	Jobs
PSLE & below	Jobs

By Employment Status	Primary Driver for Soul
Employed	Jobs
Not Employed / Dependent	Jobs

By Age	Primary Driver for Soul
15–24	Jobs
25–39	Jobs
40–59	Community Basics
60 & above	Prosperity

By House Type	Primary Driver for Soul
1–3 room HDB	Jobs
4 room HDB	Jobs
5–exec HDB	Jobs
Private	Community Basics

relates to basic needs like Food & Shelter and Health & Wealth. For Singaporeans living in private housing, it is Community Basics in the form of Basic Infrastructure like Roads, Highways, the Public Transportation System, the Educational System and aspects of the Environment like the quality of air, water and the beauty of our physical settings.

CONCLUSION

In conclusion, what is the big picture? I think we need to forge new paths. We need new flying instruments, and we need new concepts like Population Segments, Engaged Citizenry, Citizen Relationship Management; and we need different strokes for different folks. In the last decade or so, social scientists and talent cartographers like Richard Florida have told us that the world is "spiky", that the most talented and mobile will trend toward cities and communities where they can best put their talents to their best use every single day, where they can continuously achieve their goals in their work and lives, and where they can provide and ensure the very best of environment for their families and loved ones. Gallup's research, past and current, supports this hypothesis. Countries, cities and communities with high psychological capital and social capital in addition to good national, financial, and community infrastructure will be better able to attract, engage and retain the very best talents, especially those who are highly mobile. And these talents will lead the way in creating the next wave of innovation, creativity, business and economic success, and the sustainability of that success.

Already, Singapore plays at the apex of the world's stage in all aspects of national, financial and community infrastructure. Moving forward, for Singapore to further move up the food chain and be a super strong magnet for talents and businesses foreign and local, we must create a very high sense of Soul, Engaged Citizenry, Personal Expression and Well-Being on our shores, for all Singaporeans. We must create and build a very high sense of psychological and social capital. What do I mean? We need all segments of our Singapore population to flourish as best as they can, and for as many Singaporeans as we can to exhibit high psychological capital like hope, optimism, resiliency and self-efficacy. We also need high social capital in Singapore. Neighbour looking after neighbour. A caring, cohesive, civic minded spirit exhibited across our entire society. A strong spirit of giving back to society such that society and the city get better and stronger time after time. Cities and communities with high social capital have strong alignment, high community harmony, a healthy sense of civic-mindedness, integration, cohesion, and most importantly, the pride and passion in its citizens very much like the engaged citizen model we have just talked about.

Psychological and Social Capital are important concepts for Singapore to leverage and ace in our next lap. We need every Singaporean to be highly engaged, and to exhibit a strong sense of pride and passion for our country. When we are able to do so, combined with the outstanding success we have already attained in our national, financial and community infrastructure, we will be able to predict, with a high degree of confidence, Singapore's success into the next millennium. That, I believe, is the Heart of the Matter.

CHAPTER 3

Trust and Let Go

PHILIP JEYARETNAM

I am not an expert, just a practitioner… but I suppose the one advantage I have is that I can speak from some experience, so that is what I will try and do now. Maybe, before going on to some of that experience of my own engagement, I could try to answer that earlier question which Debra has posed, which was: Are people ready to step up to the plate?

THE TRIANGLE OF SUSPICION

I wanted just to identify something which holds us back, which holds Singapore back. I identify this as a triangle of suspicion. When I first thought of it yesterday, I thought "triangle of fear", but I thought that was a bit too strong… so, triangle of suspicion. The dynamic starts like this: when you have people of different backgrounds coming together and living in close proximity, there is a strong tendency to fear your neighbours. The different smells, the customs, the behaviour… So from there you have a natural desire that somebody out there will keep your neighbours in check, that they will follow the rules, and indeed beyond having rules and implementing them and enforcing them, that someone out there will mediate between different groups in society. And you get that natural dynamic where you have that enforcer who plays a mediating role, triangulates between disparate groups and kind of takes charge.

Now, the second apex in this triangle is a philosophy within the ruling party that suggests that political competition is not a good thing, and is even bad. So you then have a suspicion when people form associations, when people come together, you have a suspicion that they are going to become platforms for political dissent and competition.

This suspicion or philosophy then fuels or leads into the third apex of the triangle, which is citizens themselves becoming cautious about associating, for fear that this is considered to be a political act, and that they might find themselves being nipped in the bud. So, I think that explains a lot of the sense that when there is a problem, the citizen does not go out and form a cat patrol society but instead writes in to the forum page of the newspaper.

Obviously, real progress on this front does depend on breaking this vicious triangle. But I would suggest that it is important to do so, and it is important to do so, because I think the old mantra that Singapore was too small for people to "rock the boat" needs to be replaced by a new idea, a new sense that Singapore is too small **not** to let people row their own boats, if that is what they want to do, not to let people change mid-stream if that is what they want to do.

PRINCIPLE OR EFFICIENCY?

Let me then just pull it back to something which I have experienced. There are a number of things I could talk about, but I thought the most obvious would perhaps be the legal profession, because that is what I spend most of my time doing, and I have that experience of having been the President of the Law Society for four years from 2003 to 2007.

The legal profession is obviously a source of social capital. It is a network that strengthens society, *et cetera, et cetera*, and so the question of how the legal profession is regulated is an important one. I just want to draw out from the experience of the profession the importance of considering principle as well as considering effectiveness. Sometimes when we look at this question of whether the government can do less, and people do more, we try to answer the question only in terms of, well, which is the better way of delivering the goods? Is it more effective for kidney dialysis to be the preserve of the Ministry of Health, which is a tax-funded service, or is it better for it to be a matter for the charitable private sector? And we consider it in these terms, in terms of effectiveness rather than necessarily in terms of principle.

Now, the legal profession provides us with a clear iteration of the principle that you need 'protected space' for society to thrive. The legal profession shows this most particularly because the legal profession is the bedrock of the independence of the judiciary. It is an absolute given that Singapore requires an independent judiciary for it to succeed economically. But perhaps what has not always been appreciated so clearly, and one of the things I had to spend a lot of time articulating as President was that an independent judiciary depends on an independent legal profession. When you regulate the profession you have to make sure you are not undermining or reducing that independence. There may be lots of laudable efficiency goals. You may think it is faster to regulate centrally by government, but you lose something very valuable, which is that you cannot have an independent judiciary without an independent profession, without people knowing they can be represented fearlessly by lawyers even when they are up against the state.

Let me just say that the Law Society is independent. Nobody gives instructions to anyone in the Council about what to do. But unfortunately — perhaps because of history — there is an impression that might linger and that makes it harder for the Law Society to meet its full potential, and for the legal profession to meet its full potential, because of changes that took place in the past. In particular, in the 1980s there was a serious misstep in my opinion. First of all, the Minister for Law was given the power to appoint three out of the Society's 20 Council members. Secondly, there were the changes to Section 38(1)(c) of the Legal Profession Act to not allow the Law Society to comment on legislation unless the changes have been submitted to it first.

I will just explain a little bit about both of those very quickly. When we talk about appointments by the Minister for Law, I am certainly not quarrelling with the tremendous quality that those appointees have, and the contributions that they have made. They have been fantastic. In fact, one should not generalise but if anything, they have been even more hardworking than some other members of Council who are already very hardworking. Second thing I should say is that in Singapore, "what you see is what you get". If the statute says the Minister has the power to appoint, that is all it means. The members of the Council who are appointed by government do not report back, and do not take instructions.

Can the profession not be left on its own to elect its leadership? Do appointments — even of a small number — made by the political executive not undermine the principle of independence of the legal profession? This is an important point. It makes it difficult for us when we interact with other Bar associations, not just those in developed nations but even in places like China, where the regional Bar associations are telling you that government appointments to their governing bodies are being reduced or eliminated, and then they wonder why we still have three appointments when we are such an advanced nation. Is it really necessary? If it is only a matter of perception, then is it not time to do away with it?

At the same time, we have to ask, why do we need Section 38(1)(c)? Section 38(1)(c) stipulates that the Law Society can only assist the government on legislation submitted to us. Well, I can understand that you do not want Bar associations entering politics. But the question really is, who should be deciding where the boundaries are? Is this a matter for lawmakers or politicians, or is this a matter for society as a whole? Can you not actually leave it to professional associations or other non-governmental organisations (NGOs) to decide the boundaries themselves? Maybe there will be some mistakes, but probably most of the time they will get it right, and they will get to exercise power responsibly. But if you do not even provide that space, then you are actually short-changing the professions in terms of their potential.

I think we should avoid the fallacy of thinking that that funding from the state can only happen when the entity is state-controlled, and that civil society or that protected space has to be free of state funding. I think that is misconceived. Technically, taxpayers' money is taxpayers' money... when we say that is government money, I think that is actually shorthand for taxpayers' money. And who are the taxpayers? The entire society, including civil society. What the state has, of course, is that power of raising funds from the population at large. So I think there is no contradiction in private initiatives getting public funding, and obviously in the situation of the arts, it is essential... you actually must take that position, that the arts will both be free and receive some degree of state support. The two things actually go hand-in-hand.

But I do understand the underbelly of that, which is the fear of the lack of accountability, and therefore the need to keep an eye on where the money is going, if you are funding something. But again, I would answer that by saying it is not quite right to say that all accountability is via government, via the state. People can hold associations to account directly, and there is also the role of the media. The media has played this role effectively to date: in Singapore notably in the last few years, for example, the National Kidney Foundation has been held to account.

BUILDING TRUST AND PARTNERSHIPS

As I pointed out in my introduction, we are the last man standing, we are the last independently regulated profession in Singapore. Let me just end with this. I will give an example that might alarm some and hearten others. The Australian Law Council is, I think, a remarkable institution. This is shown in the case of Mohamed Haneef, an Indian doctor who happened to have links with, who occasionally corresponded by email with one of his cousins who was one of the July bombers in London. He was arrested in Australia. It was pure guilt by association. The Australian Law Council was first off the bat saying, this is wrong. They were proven right. That is a remarkable thing, when you have even opposition parties in Australia not seeing the rule-of-law issue so clearly, the Australia Law Council was able to move so quickly. That to me is an amazing thing, for it shows the strength and the resilience of the legal profession and what it can contribute to society.

History has proved them right, but what if they had made a mistake? Well, so what, really? But that is an example of the benefits of the protected space for professional and other associations can provide. I really think that we have reached the stage in our development where we cannot afford not to have that degree of protected space, that degree of contribution from citizens and citizens banding together. If I had to sum it up, this is an area where collectively we need to think big, not just make small changes, and build trust and partnerships, in place of suspicion.

CHAPTER 4

Information, Insulation and the Public Interest

CHERIAN GEORGE

Democracy encourages us to believe in the ideal of the sovereign and competent citizen; one who pays attention to public affairs and bases his decisions on a thorough appraisal of the options facing his society. This ideal may be lofty but it is unrealistic, says one critic. It is an unattainable ideal and, therefore, bad, "in the sense that is it bad for a fat man to try to be a ballet dancer". "An ideal should express the true possibilities of its subject," he says. Really, individuals do not know what's going on in public affairs, he adds. "I cannot imagine how he could know, and there is not the least reason for thinking, as mystical democrats have thought, that the compounding of individual ignorance in masses of people can produce a continuous directing force in public affairs."

This dose of hard truth could have been dispensed straight from MM Lee Kuan Yew's medicine chest. In fact, these are the views of Walter Lippmann, one of America's most respected public intellectuals in 20th century. Lippmann argued that the belief that each citizen must acquire "a competent opinion about all public affairs" is an "intolerable and unworkable fiction". He said that while citizens had to have the power to elect their government, the routine work of government had to be guided by special expertise. His prescription was an "independent, expert organization" — a kind of super think-tank — that would advise government officials as well as interpret public affairs for the layman and the press.[1]

Lippmann's concern reminds us that anxieties about policy and public opinion are nothing new, and not peculiar to Singapore. It may be particularly timely to examine it here and now, given the government's concern since the 2011 General Election (GE) that cyberspace was full of "many negative views and ridiculous untruths" that could lead people astray, as Prime Minister Lee Hsien Loong warned in his 2011 National Day Rally Speech. But this problem pre-dates Facebook and Twitter and even older technologies like television, the telephone and telegraph. It goes to the heart of one of democratic theory's greatest dilemmas. Although it is obvious that the democratic one-man-one-vote system cannot function without an informed electorate, the question that has yet to be resolved is what is the reasonable level of "informedness" that we should expect of the public, and whether and how we can achieve it.

All electoral democracies face the risk that the sum of individual choices will not add up to collective well-being. Individuals can fail to act in their own best interests by foregoing long-term security for short-term palliatives. Even when fully cognisant of their own interests, citizens can neglect considering the interests of others. Democratic systems address these risks in two ways: by improving the flow of information to and among citizens in the expectation that a better informed electorate will have a greater chance of arriving at the common good; and insulating certain spheres of decision-making from democratic choice, on the grounds that these are better left to experts — the rule of law, for example, requires that the judicial system is shielded from the vagaries of public opinion. Every democracy employs a mix of both strategies — information and insulation — but the balance between the two, and the precise approaches taken, differ from society to society.

SINGAPORE'S APPROACH

Singapore's resolution of this dilemma is itself the result of two distinct and apparently contradictory convictions. On the one hand is its belief in being

---

[1] Walter Lippmann (1992). *Public Opinion*. New York: Macmillan; Walter Lippmann (1925). *The Phantom Public*. New York: New York University Press.

forthright with the people — often in exhaustive, repetitive detail. In contrast to the fantasies that are routinely peddled by leaders in many other countries, the PAP (People's Action Party) has a tradition of being brutally honest about Singapore's challenges, limitations and vulnerabilities. In the world of political speechmaking, our National Day Rallies, for example, are unusually sombre and didactic events.

On the other hand, this communicative compulsion is counter-balanced by a deep-seated pessimism about the public's potential to rise to the challenge of democratic citizenship. In common with theorists of democratic elitism such as Walter Lippmann, the PAP believes that democracy needs to be protected from itself — that beyond a point, public participation is destabilising. It believes that in some areas, decisions are simply too technical for the masses to grasp; in others, the gulf between short-term individual interests and long-term societal interests too cavernous for most people's minds to bridge; while some issues are too visceral to expect people to exercise cool rationality.

The PAP's low expectations of the public are seen in Singapore's broadcasting policies. When the government progressively loosened the leash around the neck of the national broadcaster in the 1980s, the stations were not asked to emulate the BBC-style independent public service model. Instead, in line with the market fetishism of the times, policy-makers decided that TV was inevitably about show business. This is significant because international research has shown that the level of basic political knowledge in a society — the kind of awareness that we expect citizens to have — is closely related to the strength of public service broadcasting. Current debates in Singapore are obsessed about the internet, but we have probably not looked hard enough at the three decades of television policy, which may have been the single most powerful cultural factor behind cultivating an entire generation of Singaporeans as consumers of public services instead of citizens with a right and responsibilities to participate in public life.

The Singapore strategy thus far has been to develop a public opinion that can be trusted to follow wise leadership, but not attempt to take the lead. The latest iteration of this elitist approach is presented as reaction to a deep concern about the irrational and anarchic forces that run riot in social media, but the underlying logic is several decades old. Once upon a time,

31

the stumbling block was said to be Singapore's lowly-educated population, new to their civic responsibilities in a modern, independent city state. Later, it was the overwhelming ideological influence of great powers, whether in the liberal west or the communist east. Now, it is the confusion and disaffection sown by irresponsible individuals in cyberspace. Always, the narrative puts people in their place, a place where the common good is just beyond their reach and would never be grasped, but for the assistance of a small and able team of gifted men and women.

INFORMATION GAPS

Over the decades, nonetheless, PAP leaders have acknowledged that they must meet the growing demands for information and explanation from a better-educated and more skeptical population. Last year's GE has pushed this trend further. The government is now convinced that making its presence felt in social media will reap dividends. On their own, though, such efforts will probably fail to achieve the desired result. There will always be gaps between policy — what the state believes is for the common good — and public opinion — what people believe is in their interest. In some cases, it is because we are dealing with public goods. While there seems to be wide support for National Service (NS), we are probably wise not to trust NS to individual choice but to make conscription inescapable. As a country, we recognise that no amount of education about the need for NS can fully erase the free rider problem. Information helps, but we ultimately need compulsion, and this has not been politically controversial.

In some other cases, we've seen how information can dramatically close the gap. The government's handling of the SARS (Severe Acute Respiratory Syndrome) crisis is a textbook case. The question is whether the communication conundrum facing the PAP right now is SARS-like: whether the solution is to be found in a high-intensity information campaign, crowding out other voices by sheer dominance of public space. Perhaps some challenges are, but most are not.

Consider the most controversial policies in the GE: immigration, public transport, housing prices, and ministerial salaries. On all these issues, people had ample opportunity to hear the government's arguments before and during the GE. Are we to believe that if only politicians had used Facebook and other social media earlier and more enthusiastically, communication would have improved and the vote would have been kinder to the PAP? I am incredulous. Similarly, it is hard to accept that, if only Singapore's establishment media had conveyed government positions with even greater fidelity than they did, the gap between government and people would have been narrowed. Increased communicativeness will be more persuasive only if the context — the communication environment — changes. The element in the communication environment that is critically lacking, without which any additional communicativeness would be futile, is trust.

In the past, the PAP counted mainly on its track record and charismatic leadership to engender that trust. This is no longer possible. The demands on government have become more complex, making it harder to satisfy all of the people all of the time. Furthermore, since the Old Guard leadership passed the baton to new generation leaders, the emphasis has been on technocratic ability. Successive PAP slates have had many positive attributes, but charisma is not one that immediately comes to mind.

TRUST DEFICIT

There appear to be three barriers to building trust. First, the primary platform through which government communicates with the public, the mainstream media, suffers from a credibility problem. In most areas of coverage, the media are professional enough to provide a valued and reliable service, including on most routine government news. However, at any one time, there are issues on which media credibility is low. The number of such issues may be small, but they are precisely the ones with the largest potential gap between policy and public opinion.

In such circumstances, government media policy dictates that the independent professional judgment of editors must be subordinate to elected officials' judgments. The press is expected to educate the public and rally the nation behind the government, rather than push the government to respond to the people. What this effectively means is that the media are required to manage, muffle and mute public discontent while affirming and amplifying the government view. On all the election hot-button issues, public discontent was never totally covered up by the media, but people never got the sense that the media were on their side. And this severely limits the power of the media to guide the public precisely where that influence is most needed.

Second, the communication environment lacks independent voices in public debates: state and non-state institutions that stand apart from the executive, with the competence and credibility to comment authoritatively on problems and policies. These could include Ombudsmen, Commissions, independent think-tanks and other non-partisan expert institutions.

This is where the PAP differs from the theorists like Lippmann. Democratic elitism — whose proponents have included Samuel Huntingdon and Joseph Schumpeter as well as Lippmann — places its faith in a plural and competitive elite. PAP philosophy has not been enamoured of such intra-elite checks and balances because of the fear that these will slow down governance and confuse the public. These risks are small relative to the benefits, in the form of the increased trust that could accrue to the government when more of its decisions are subject to independent scrutiny by competent institutions. Singaporeans have come to expect such oversight in all areas of life where we ourselves cannot hope to muster the necessary expertise.

Finally, there is the problem of conflict of interest, between national interest and party interest. While there is significant overlap between the interests of the ruling party and the interests of Singapore, these interests are not coterminous and most Singaporeans can see that. The most obvious example is the way electoral boundaries are drawn: the process is, beyond reasonable doubt, managed to benefit the PAP. Similarly, unequal treatment towards opposition constituencies when rolling out government programmes and services simply does not pass the smell test.

The odour of partisanship hangs in the air and sticks to other unpopular policies, even those which an objective analysis might conclude are justified as being in the national interest. Such cynicism will continue to corrode trust as long as there are specific areas in which the government has, in the eyes of any reasonable Singaporean, put party before nation. Building trust in the communication environment is critically important because, like it or not, theories of democratic elitism have a point. Citizens — even highly educated ones with an interest in public affairs — can only take so much information about policies before their eyes glaze over. Some will demand facts and figures in great detail and if the government is on firm ground, it should have no compunctions about providing the data. For most, however, it will be about taking a leap of faith, and that is where trust gives you wings. That trust cannot grow if the media are consistently forced to side with policy against public opinion 100 percent of the time, if we lack independent institutions to scrutinise the work of the executive, and if the government continues to conflate party interests with national interests.

In an earlier era, we had faith in the doctors because of the aura that the medical profession projected. Today, if we trust our doctors, it is not because we think they are gods, nor because we have studied medicine ourselves and can check their every move, but because of the assurance that our doctors function within a regulatory system that compels them to act in our interest, that the penalties if they fail to do so are high, and that we can get a second opinion if we want. Such principles should be applicable to government as well. It is not mere repetition of our leaders' diagnoses and prescriptions that will persuade the public to swallow bitter medicine, but the assurance that they will open their decisions to independent scrutiny and verification. Since we no longer expect to be led by gods, proof of fallibility is not a liability. On the contrary, timely revelations of government's mistakes are the proof we need that we are operating in a trustworthy communication environment. Conversely, if our institutions are only capable of telling us that the government is right, it should not be surprising that they are not believed.

Think tanks are supposed to think the unthinkable, and it is in this spirit that I have offered these comments. My prescription amounts to instituting limits on government and party, and the PAP has always operated on the principle of unlimited government in a dominant-party system. These ideas might be thinkable if the ship of state was in the dock, ready for an overhaul. But one of the ironies of Singapore's success story is that because the ship is still cruising, it is that much harder to repair it. Asking the PAP to countenance a more competitive politics may be, to borrow Lippmann's metaphor, like asking a fat man to be a ballet dancer. Whether it is unthinkable for a fat man to lose his extra pounds without losing himself is a question I will leave you with.

CHAPTER 5

Model Of Governance: Big Government or Big People?

PETER HO

BIG GOVERNMENT

Small government, the opposite of big government, is aimed at reducing the role of the state in the economy. In taking a *laissez-faire* approach towards regulating the private sector, it is argued that small government lowers costs and promotes efficiency by allowing the market to determine prices and economic outcomes. Margaret Thatcher was a champion of small government.

But small government has not been seen as an unqualified success. Critics have cited increased costs of public services, unemployment, and a widening wealth gap, as some of the unintended consequences of small government.

So is the opposite of small government — big government — the better approach? After the 2008 global financial crisis that many blame on unfettered greed and dysfunction in the private sector, we see evidence that the tide of public opinion is turning against small government. So the jury is out and the debate will continue.

GOVERNMENT IN SINGAPORE

What sort of government do we have in Singapore? Is it small government — or is it big government?

Depending on whom one asks, different commentators will offer different views on the "size" and influence of Singapore's government.

Some analysts see our government as exercising "big" or substantial influence. It exercises jurisdiction not just over traditional areas of policy, like defence, macroeconomics and infrastructure, but also in areas like tree-planting and compulsory savings which are seen as more municipal or personal in other countries. The ban on the sale of chewing gum has been cited by many as an example of a pervasive and intrusive government role.

On other measures, Singapore's government is not particularly big.

The Washington think tank, the Heritage Foundation, together with the *Wall Street Journal*, compiles an annual "Index of Economic Freedom" measuring several dimensions of a country's economic freedom.

One of these dimensions is the size of government spending, which in Singapore has been relatively low. According to the most recent Index of Economic Freedom, total government expenditure in Singapore, including consumption and transfer payments, constituted 17 per cent of Gross Domestic Product (GDP).

This is one of the lowest in the world. In comparison, Hong Kong's total government expenditure amounted to 18.6 per cent of GDP, and it does not have to spend on defence. In the United States, such expenditure totalled 38.9 per cent of GDP. In Australia, it was 34.3 per cent, and in New Zealand, 41.1 per cent.

THE PARADOX OF GOVERNMENT

There is a paradox of government that I discovered after many years in the public service. The law of diminishing returns applies to government as much as it does to economics. The marginal return on government policies diminishes over time, even as the effort to implement policy stays constant or even increases.

I surmise that there are a couple of reasons for this. The first reason is that as government policies lead to improvements, the needs of the people change. This is explained by Abraham Maslow's Hierarchy of Needs, a theory in psychology advanced more than half a century ago. Maslow's proposition was that after the basic physiological needs of a person are met, more complex psychological needs will have to be fulfilled. At the top of this hierarchy of needs is the need for self-actualisation, which is to realise the individual's potential.

So if you accept this proposition, then after government has delivered on the basic needs of food, security, shelter, transport and health, expectations of the people are going to change, not in demanding more of the basic needs, but in fulfilling their more psychic needs in the upper reaches of Maslow's hierarchy, including social, emotional and self-actualisation needs.

The debate over whether Singapore should place economic growth at the centre of government policy, ideas like a national happiness index, and the demand for more participation in the political discourse and in policy-making, reflect how our needs are changing.

The second reason is what I term here the "third generation effect". Singapore is now 46 years old, and into the third generation of Singaporeans. The first generation of Singaporeans lived through the turbulence and uncertainties of Merger and Separation. The next generation started life on a firmer footing, but at the same time imbibed from their parents a sense of the vulnerabilities. But the third generation of Singaporeans have known only the affluence and success of Singapore. For them, the uncertainties of the 60s and 70s are abstractions from their school history books. When their grandparents speak of the turmoil and danger that they experienced, they shrug their shoulders because it is an experience outside theirs.

What persuaded their parents and grandparents may not work as well with the third generation. So communicating to the third generation will require fresh arguments and different approaches.

THE CHANGING ROLE OF GOVERNMENT

These and other reasons will change and transform the role of government.

In the beginning, government was characterised by strong regulation — big government if you will — seeking compliance with policy rules, and maintaining as efficient a system as possible.

But today, citizens and businesses alike have far higher expectations of government than before. Access to information has increased dramatically in scope and speed as a result of the internet revolution. Social networking platforms like blogs, Facebook, YouTube and Twitter have empowered citizens to express their views. Virtual communities are beginning to shape the debate and context of public policy issues.

The mindset of "government knows best" is irrelevant in today's world, where citizens and businesses can easily gain access to much of the information that governments used to monopolise and control in the past.

What is the appropriate model of governance for Singapore in the future? The question is not simply whether the people have a sufficient input into government policy. It is also how much we should rely on the market to decide on policy outcomes and public deliverables. How government interacts with the private and the people sectors will in turn determine how "big" a role each of these sectors will play.

BIG MARKETS

One limit on the size of our government has been our belief that free market forces should determine prices and economic outcomes. This is the approach advocated for small government.

But our faith in the market has not been uncritical or absolute. We have not been ideological about small government. Instead, we recognise that in certain cases, unfettered market forces can result in excessive volatility, negative externalities and under-provision of merit goods, like education, as well as public goods, like defence.

The economist, Dani Rodrik, outlined a framework that can be usefully applied to understanding how Singapore has chosen to blend the work of markets and the government:

- First, the government has sought to *enable markets*. This includes ensuring rule of law, property rights, and public infrastructure — functions that most governments perform. In Singapore, enabling markets has also included industrial policy and capability development, subjects of some controversy in policy circles around the world, especially among proponents of small government that believe in the *laissez-faire* approach.

- Second, the government has sought to *regulate markets*. This includes supervision of the financial sector, competition regulation, and taxation of negative externalities. But a key feature of Singapore's approach has been the shift towards lighter regulation accompanied by risk-based supervision.

- Third, the government has sought to *stabilise markets*. This is the bread-and-butter of macroeconomic management. Singapore's basic approach in monetary and fiscal policy is not far different from global practices. But its efforts to address asset price inflation and credit crises are interesting examples of targeted interventions that harness market forces.

- Fourth, the government has sought to *legitimise markets*. Globalisation, free trade, and open markets have led to significant dislocations. Some of the sharpest debates over the role of governments centre on this: to what extent should governments facilitate adjustments, redistribute incomes, or provide social safety nets, so as to maintain public support for market-oriented policies?

ENGAGING BIG SOCIETY

Complementing government and markets, we will also need a strong society — one that is robust and resilient — to tackle the great challenges of the 21st century.

These challenges will increasingly be "wicked problems" — characterised by multi-dimensionality and growing complexity. Their causes and contributing factors will not be easily identified *ex ante*. Today, the government faces an increasing number of complex public policy issues in which the trade-offs are much more difficult to make, because each could lead to unintended consequences and risks. Many of these public policy issues exceed the capacity of government working alone. Instead, they require the active contribution of private and people sectors. A government-centric approach focused on efficiency and productivity must give way to a broader focus in which government also leverages on the collective capacity of non-government actors, to achieve results of higher public value and at a lower overall cost for society.

This approach has been most evident in the economic arena. A succession of four economic reviews (The Economic Committee of 1986, the Committee on Singapore's Competitiveness of 1998, the Economic Review Committee of 2003, and the most recent Economic Strategies Committee of 2008) saw the public and private sectors coming together to produce far-reaching policy recommendations for Singapore's long-term economic competitiveness.

The coming years will see a growing need for *governance* — which requires collaboration across the public, private and people sectors — rather than *government* acting as the sole, or even dominant, player.

A key part of this governance process will be growing mutual engagement between the public and people sectors. In his 2011 National Day Rally, Prime Minister Lee Hsien Loong underscored the importance of such engagement, pointing out that the nation needs to "harness diverse views and ideas, put aside personal interest and forge common goals".

There are four broad areas where engagement will be important.

PUBLIC INFORMATION

In some cases, engagement will involve the government informing the public: providing objective information clearly and succinctly, that helps the public understand the context, alternatives and choices involved in an issue.

Traditional channels for this include fact sheets, websites, open houses, and press releases. It calls for good communication skills, such as sharing concise, specific and relevant information in a timely manner. As contexts, expectations and technologies evolve, other considerations come into play.

- First, public issues are becoming more multi-dimensional and complex.
- Second, mobile technologies now allow busy but tech-savvy citizenry to stay connected.
- Third, a more educated and connected public expects greater openness and transparency from government. "Government knows best" responses are likely to alienate the public; and, in an environment where no one has all the answers, can they hold true.

Efforts to inform the public will need to take into account these developments as well as prevailing social behaviours in order to maximise their reach and impact.

PUBLIC CONSULTATION

A second form of engagement is public consultation, which involves gathering ideas and feedback from the public on analysis or proposals by the government, so that the public's perspectives, concerns and aspirations can be taken into consideration.

Over the years, a number of channels have been established for public consultation in Singapore. The Feedback Unit, today called REACH, organises focus group dialogues. Government agencies are beginning to use social networking tools to extend their reach to connect with citizens, in spite of uncertainties, unknowns — and even risks — involved. Some of our government ministers now discuss their respective ministry's plans and thinking through blogs. Agencies conduct their own consultation exercises and web-based surveys to solicit the public's inputs on proposed policy amendments, or seek ideas on service design.

An example of this was the Ministry of Health's (MOH) work on means-testing in healthcare. In a series of dialogue sessions, MOH officers distilled and used the learning from each dialogue to refine the policy, then tested the new ideas out at the next session. Dialogues to seek citizens' views on the pegging of subsidy rates were reported in the media. As more understood the rationale for change, support for it grew.

CONSENSUS-BUILDING

A third form of engagement is to partner the public in framing issues, developing alternatives and building consensus on preferred solutions.

Such consensus is achieved through deliberation and dialogue that help to deepen understanding, reframe and define issues, promote clarity and reach agreement. Decision-making could be jointly made by the government and the public, or in specific cases devolved to the public.

Examples include inter-religious and tripartite labour dialogues, where potentially divisive issues are debated and deliberated behind closed doors and an alignment of positions is sought before a unified stand is announced to the public.

With greater social diversity, increased complexity and demands for transparency, more public issues will become contentious in future. More conversations may need to be selectively extended into the public space to deepen collective understanding, and build society's capacity to deliberate issues rationally in a safe environment.

An example of such consensus-building is the Land Transport Authority's (LTA) efforts to work with communities. In some private estates, for instance, LTA worked with grassroots leaders to facilitate a dialogue so residents could voice their concerns. Together, they agreed on a traffic scheme to optimise roadside parking spaces in the estate. Residents then helped to enforce the scheme by reporting infringements.

CO-CREATION

In some instances, a fourth form of engagement is to involve community in the co-creation of policies. This can engender greater ownership of outcomes and increase overall public value beyond what any single sector can achieve on its own.

The "Community in Bloom" programme, initiated by the National Parks Board and People's Association to foster a love for gardening and promote community bonding, is an example of such collaboration between the government and people. Other stories of co-creation include rehabilitating and reintegrating ex-offenders into society, promoting environmental awareness and protection, and neighbourhood policing.

THE FUTURE OF BIG SOCIETY

This chapter has deliberately spent some time deliberating how society can evolve, and how government can play a role in that. This has not been an area where Singapore has had extensive experience. It means a shift from "government to you" and "government for you", to "government with you". The imperative is for government to move towards a collaborative approach to policy-making, and be prepared to co-create and connect with the people.

Engagement will not always be possible, of course. Some aspects of policymaking, like tax rates, exchange rate levels, and defence or foreign policies will rightly continue to be determined by technical experts.

However, the role of society will certainly grow, which will be welcomed as Singapore navigates the new challenges we face as a nation in the 21st century. These challenges will require our government, markets and society to all become bigger than they used to be.

CHAPTER 6

Governance in Singapore: History and Legacy

CHAN HENG CHEE

INTRODUCTION

History to a large extent explains why countries have particular political traditions, why they hold certain values dear and why they develop characteristic responses and reflexes. Over time, countries and people develop habits of the heart and of the mind.

There is the American political model with identifiable American values and reflexes, and even though administrations change and different parties take over, the American political model remains and the political reflexes are quite predictable. The Second Amendment to the American Constitution introduced in 1791 spells out the right to bear arms. Today, after so many cases of shootings in schools and a groundswell of anti-gun feelings, it is still difficult to take away that right. The gun lobby is strong and the current American President, Barack Obama and all those who want to do something about the senseless killings can only talk about outlawing specific types of guns and introducing more stringent checks, and even that is pushed back. Now President Obama is talking about using a presidential decree to push through a new law.

There is the Chinese Communist model. The Chinese Communist Party (CCP) underwent change with Deng Xiaoping's "Four Modernisations" — ideology weakened, some would say evaporated, but the Party remains strong. Many of the reflexes and traditions remain.

But change does occur and must occur as a country develops, and this is sometimes a rapid fundamental change. America had its counterculture revolution triggered by the Vietnam War. There were some major social value changes, especially with the women's movement and Black Power, where existing authority structures were profoundly challenged and questioned. There was significant social change, and even though there was change in the political culture too, the political and governing model remained more or less the same. The first African–American president was only elected in 2008. Change in political model seems to lag behind change in political culture.

I go into some length about the United States (US) because it is a country I have come to know, and I find it helpful to reflect on other countries when thinking about history and political change in Singapore.

Then, there are revolutions like the Arab Spring that can disrupt a model and overthrow institutions. Revolutions are often followed by a period of adjustment that is often long and difficult, but even then, some core values and reflexes can resurface.

"SINGAPORE EXCEPTIONALISM"

Every country claims exceptionalism. President Obama reminded Americans that when they think of themselves as an exceptional country and talk of "American exceptionalism" they should remember the French too claim exceptionalism, and there is "German exceptionalism", "South African exceptionalism", and so on.

I would like to speak of "Singapore exceptionalism", for in many ways we are an exceptional country. I say this not to be proud or arrogant, but to recognise that we are *sui generis* — unique, of its own kind. We are an unlikely nation, the only city-state that is also nation-state in the world. We are a micro-state and one that has developed to its furthest, the strategy of small state survival. We did not have to develop this way: a successful country with a record of enviable growth for more than four decades. It could have gone the other way. Americans tell me all the time that we are a small country that gets things done. When we say we will do something, we do it — for instance, how many times have we reformed the education system hoping each time to make it better? Foreign diplomats in Singapore marvel at the way Singapore and Singaporeans have a "can do" mentality.

Some frankly say that in their countries they spend so much time arguing about things that nothing or very little gets implemented in the end.

(An aside: I just read in an Economist Intelligence Unit or EIU global survey in which people were asked which country they would want to be born in, Singapore ranked number six. All the Nordic countries ranked near the top. EIU concluded that people wanted to be born in a country that is small, peaceful and homogeneous and a liberal democracy, but Singapore surprised them completely.[1])

Why is Singapore the way it is? What is the political model we have developed? What are our governing reflexes and national shared values? In Singapore, and after the 2011 General Election, there is a great deal of talk about the change needed. There are those who focus on the policy changes they would like to see. But there is a segment that wants to see change in the political model — into a Western-style democracy with a two-party system.

This chapter reflects on the Singapore situation: what we are, why we are what we are and where we will be heading.

SINGAPORE'S HISTORY AND LEGACY

I began by setting out how historical circumstances shape values, tradition and governing models. Let me quickly go through some historical facts to make a few points. In 1965, Singapore achieved independence unexpectedly. Survival was the issue, front and centre. Singaporeans could feel it. What would our future be? What next? We had no natural resources except for our people and our location. No oil, no minerals, no forests, no water and not much airspace. We had just lost our hinterland. We were not a normal country. Moreover, the immediate regional context was a hostile one. Separation from Malaysia was accompanied by explosive racial rhetoric and sentiments. Indonesia under Sukarno was pursuing *Konfrontasi* against Singapore and Malaysia, complete with commando landings. We were at our most vulnerable.

---

[1] See the Economic Intelligence Unit's 'The where-to-be-born index 2013'.

The Singapore government defined its first task as ensuring the territorial and economic survival of the country. The defence and foreign policy emphasised Singapore as a non-aligned country but accommodated the British bases because of the security context, and within a matter of two years, together with Indonesia, Malaysia, Thailand and the Philippines, we formed the Association of Southeast Asian Nations (ASEAN). So right from the start, we established Singapore as an independent, non-aligned country that is more pro-West and that believes in multilateralism and regional groupings as the way forward.

To build the economy, Prime Minister (PM) Lee Kuan Yew, cabinet ministers and civil servants went around the world securing foreign investments. They learned that political stability was the first condition foreign investors requested. In the 1950s and 1960s, Singapore went through a period of contentious politics of student riots, strikes and racial riots. Political debate was heated and passionate in the battle for merger, followed by volatile racial politics during this period. For our leaders of that generation, Lee Kuan Yew, Goh Keng Swee, S. Rajaratnam and Toh Chin Chye, of the People's Action Party (PAP), establishing political stability was the first order of the day. I recall PM Lee's words to the trade unions at that time, "don't kill the goose that lays the golden egg". Pragmatism was a lesson we learnt out of necessity. There was a sense of grave urgency, almost an emergency, to get the economy going.

The *Barisan Sosialis*, the largest opposition party, took the decision to boycott the first Parliamentary Elections of 1968 because they declared Singapore's independence was a "phony independence". It turned out to be a historical mistake. Once out, it was hard for the opposition to come back in. It was not till 1981 that J.B. Jeyaratnam won back a seat for the opposition in the Anson by-election. So without even working for it, the PAP got its first one-party parliament. They found it was quicker to implement policies and get necessary things done to respond quickly to emerging challenges to Singapore. And there were many. British withdrawal came earlier than expected, in 1971 rather than mid-1970s. This affected defence and jobs. There was a sense in the first-generation leaders that "life is tough, we are vulnerable, we don't have many options." The governing party played hard to maintain their one-party dominance, but they delivered on their performance. High growth was maintained, jobs were created, National Service was introduced, education expanded, and Singapore's home ownership policy was launched. Singaporeans gave the PAP government their support election after election.

The political model fostered was one that facilitated quick policy-making and implementation. It rested on a dominant one-party system, promoting consensus and an overall depoliticisation of issues. In my earlier writings, I described ours as an administrative state, an authoritarian government. But it was "soft authoritarianism" — soft compared to the Republic of Korea and Taiwan, which were hard military regimes. There was clear leadership from PM Lee Kuan Yew, aided by a strong bureaucracy with technocratic emphasis. Institutions were built to invite grassroots participation — Citizens' Consultative Committees, Town Councils, feedback sessions, etc. And there was criticism that the feedback flowed up but the policies did not change. Singapore's democracy is based on the Westminster model but is not an exact copy. Fareed Zakaria described Singapore as an "illiberal democracy". We have regular and free elections but not the freedoms he expects of a liberal democracy.[2] I have described Singapore as a "tight democracy". After the 2011 General Election and the by-elections, it is getting less tight and is moving towards a normal democracy.

From the beginning, PAP leaders enumerated specific values that were considered fundamental if we were to survive as a nation. These were, and still remain, respect for multi-racialism, multi-lingualism and multi-religions, which implies that seditious attacks on any race, language or religion will not be tolerated; maintenance of law and order; meritocracy; and non-corruption. Belief in meritocracy and respect for multi-racialism, multi-lingualism and multi-religions had a critical meaning in 1965. It differentiated us from Malaysia, from which we separated. They were two visions of a nation and Separation was about the contest of the two visions: equality of the races or preferential treatment for one ethnic group. Singaporeans have embraced these values, though now and again, there is criticism that the implementation falls short of the ideal. Singaporeans expect the government to deliver on these values. These have become our

---

[2] See Zakaria, F, "The Future of Freedom. *Illiberal Democracy at Home and Abroad*", New York: W. W. Norton & Company Inc, pp. 85–86.

national values. For sure, Singaporeans would not tolerate living in a disorderly and chaotic country where law and order is weak. There is a debate going on right now about meritocracy and its unintended consequences. Yet, I do not think you will get Singaporeans to agree on dropping that principle because any alternative would be worse. We debate to make implementation better. On the economic front, given our constraints in size and the small population base, Singapore had to be an open economy, linked to the world. We have no hinterland, and in 1972 S. Rajaratnam in a flash of brilliance said, "the world will be our hinterland". So we grasped the idea of being a global city in the 1970s before globalisation became a buzzword.

Over the years, the PAP leaders have modified their political style, but not the political model. It was a paradigm that worked. PM Goh Chok Tong's leadership style was more approachable and different from PM Lee Kuan Yew. PM Lee Hsien Loong has evolved his own style — part compassion, part firm leadership. With both leaders after Lee Kuan Yew, Singapore's political space opened up gradually. The success of the governing model and its policies is reflected in the positive changes in our population. So the ground has changed and expectations have changed.

The census data between 1970 and 2010 show Singapore's demographics have been reshaped. Singaporeans are better-educated, university-educated, overseas-educated and holding better jobs. The success of PAP policies over time was game-changing. Compare the education profile of the population in 1970, 2000 and 2010 in the tables below.

Table 1 Resident population aged 10 years and over, by highest qualification attained (%), 1970

Year	1970
No qualification	28.6
Primary	37.2
Secondary	29.8
Upper Secondary	2.7
Tertiary	1.3

Table 2 Resident non-student population aged 15 years and over, by highest qualification attained (%), 2000, 2010

Year	2000	2010
Total	100.0	100.0
Below Secondary	42.6	32.4
Secondary	24.6	18.9
Post-Secondary (Non-tertiary)	9.9	11.1
Diploma & Professional Qualification	11.1	14.8
University	11.7	22.8
Total Tertiary (Diploma, Professional Qualification or University)	22.8	37.6

Table 3 Working persons by occupation

	1970		2000		2010	
Occupation	Number	%	Number	%	Number	%
Total	650,892	100	1,482,579	100	1,898,042	100
Professional & Technical (1970)	56,080	8.6	-	-	-	-
Professionals (2000, 2010)	-	-	150,265	10.1	272,083	14.3
Associate Professionals and Technicians (2000, 2010)	-	-	283,361	19.1	434,850	22.9
Administrative & Managerial (1970)	15,476	2.4	-	-	-	-
Senior Officials and Managers (2000, 2010)	-	-	211,835	14.3	249,980	13.2
Total Classified as PMET	71,556	11	645,461	43.5	956,913	50.4
Others	579,336	89	837,118	56.5	941,129	49.6
Clerical	82,941	12.7	213,588	14.4	241,830	12.7
Sales (1970)	102,628	15.8	-	-	-	-
Services (1970)	88,744	13.6	-	-	-	-
Service & Sales Workers (2000, 2010)	-	-	182,966	12.3	252,606	13.3
Agricultural Workers & Fishermen	26,943	4.1	1,158	0.1	1,009	0.1

Table 3 (Continued)

Occupation	1970		2000		2010	
	Number	%	Number	%	Number	%
Total	650,892	100	1,482,579	100	1,898,042	100
Production & Related Workers (1970) Production Craftsmen & Related Workers (2000, 2010)	254,949	39.2	106,753	7.2	102,437	5.4
Plant & Machine Operators and Assemblers (2000, 2010)	-	-	178,752	12.1	151,579	8.0
Cleaners, Labourers & Related Workers (2000, 2010)	-	-	101,149	6.8	130,332	6.9
Not Classifiable	23,131	3.6	52,752	3.6	61,334	3.2

Sources for Tables 1, 2, 3: Census of Population, 1970, 1980, 2000, 2010 and Yearbook of Statistics 2012, Department of Statistics, Republic of Singapore.

The population with tertiary education in Singapore in 2010 was 37.6% and for those in the age group 25–34 years, 70.7% had acquired tertiary education meaning that they attained diplomas and professional qualifications or attended universities.

In 2000, of those at the university level, the proportion of those who studied at local universities and overseas ones was 48% (local) and 52% (overseas). In 2010, it was 52% local and 48% overseas.

POST 2011 GE

The general election of May 2011 was a watershed. A critical mass of voters sent a message to the governing party. They want a stronger opposition presence in parliament. The popular vote went 60.1% for the PAP and 39.9% for the opposition parties. More than one in four voters were in the 21–34 age group and about 8.5% of the electorate were first-time voters.[3] There were issues — rising cost of living, inflation, income inequality, and

---

[3] These figures are found in Chang, R, "Survey of young voters: Cost of living is top concern of GEN Y", *The Straits Times*, 16 April 2011.

the influx of foreigners that is perceived to be causing job displacement and the lowering of wages particularly within the PMET (Professionals, Managerial, Executive and Technicians) sector of the workforce.

The social media revolution gave voice to and amplified the dissatisfaction and opposition views. Singaporeans are now more vocal, more demanding of their rights and they want their views heard. They have lost their fear for speaking up and voting for the opposition. Politics has become competitive again. The political culture has transformed. Singaporeans have been repoliticised.

The ruling party responded swiftly. They were in a listening mode. They recognised the social contract had broken down and they would have to build a new consensus if they were to win back support to continue with its dominance. In introducing the public engagement process in mid-2012 called "Our Singapore Conversation", the government is seeking to provide an avenue for the broader public to express their political views and aspirations, and not just the politically active or social media savvy. The Conversation has shown that different people are asking for different things and sometimes they are contradictory. It has to be a negotiated consensus. PM Lee on 25 November 2012 clarified to PAP party activists:

> "We are not just asking people, 'what are your views and I will go and I will be your note-taker and speak on your behalf'. I think we have ideals, we have ideas, we have policies and we have proposals. And it is our responsibility to lead that discussion together with people in order to persuade people to see things more in the way we do."

I think the PAP knows it has to find a new balance. But it faces a classic dilemma: do you get rid of a model and a set of policies that have worked and in many ways continue to be relevant? The basic existential context of Singapore has not changed. The vulnerabilities are still there though they may be in a different form. Today the challenge is not about survival but about remaining competitive or risking irrelevance. And policies relating to our founding values of multi-racialism, multi-lingualism and multi-religions, law and order, non-corruption, meritocracy and open economy should not be given up for we will be diminished or destroyed. These are first-order governance principles. But other aspects of governance, what I consider second-order governing principles and policies, such as that of having certificates of entitlement (COEs) to manage car-ownership, foreign talent, housing prices, transport and policies that affect the cost of living should be reviewed and improved.

CONCLUSION

I read a very good nuanced piece by Jeremy Au, a young journalist at *The Straits Times* published on 12 January 2013.[4] He wrote about politics in 2030. Au argues that "if there is a consensus about the trajectory of Singapore politics, it is that there is an unstoppable drift towards liberalisation" and for some "the true mark of Singapore's arrival is the establishment of a two-party system." But Au points out that a recent poll in the National University of Singapore of 400 students "found no clear desire among the young for a two-party system."

How long the present model of a dominant party in government will last depends on what the PAP does in terms of policies, retaining its support and recruiting good political talent with political skills into the party. It also depends on how well the opposition parties do in recruiting talent and the policies and programmes they offer. We do not know what coming challenges in the external context could impose on our political environment, but one thing is clear — Singaporeans know what the PAP has done to build-up Singapore even in the past. They do not worry about sovereignty, territorial integrity or the economic future of the country. They take all that for granted. What the bulk of the voters ask of the governing party is "what have you done for me today?" Others simply support a bigger presence of the opposition in parliament as the kind of political arrangement they want to see. So going forward, the legacy is important, but it will be a competitive fight for support.

---

[4] Au, J, "Singapore Politics 2030", *The Straits Times*, 12 January 2013.

7

Three Scenarios for Singapore's Political Future

KISHORE MAHBUBANI

There is absolutely no doubt that Singapore is going through a political transition of some kind, but I want to add that most parts of the world are also undergoing some kind of political transition. The Arab Spring is an extreme example of that. We can even look at what is going on in the United States (US) and Europe as less extreme examples. The whole world is changing.

The middle class is exploding globally, and in Asia, it is estimated to stand at 500 million people. In 2020, just seven years from now, that Asian middle class is estimated to expand by three-and-a half times to 1.75 billion. What Singapore, Asia and the rest of the world are doing now is to try to deal with the rapid and massive rise of the middle class. It is important to understand this to explain the political developments that have taken place in this region as well. This also supports Professor (Prof.) Chan Heng Chee's view of the sociological trend that is driving political change in Singapore.

I agree with the broad thesis that: "the residual" does matter. Our history and our values *do* play a part in our political trajectory. One interesting point that Prof. Chan made in Chapter 1 is that Singapore's political system was previously described as "soft authoritarianism" but, after the 2011 General Election and after the recent 2013 Punggol East by-elections, we are now a "normal democracy".

You do not go straight from a soft authoritarian system to a normal democracy. It takes time. There is a transitional process. An interesting question that we should consider today is *how* this process began and *why* it began. The best way of understanding the power of the residual element in Singapore's political culture is to project it forward, to look ahead and see where the residual will take us. None of us can predict the future. There is an Arab proverb that says, "He who speaks about the future lies and even when he tells the truth". But at the same time, as emphasised by the Institute of Policy Studies' Prism project,[1] scenario planning does help. It helps to think about alternative futures. I thought the best way of trying to figure out how the residual will play out in the future is to think of three potential scenarios that might come Singapore's way.

The first scenario, which I think is the most probable, is the soft landing from soft authoritarianism. This is what you see happening in Singapore today. We remain peaceful and prosperous. But if we are to continue to do well, we need to embrace the fundamental values that the Singapore government has emphasised from the beginning. Prof. Chan lays them out in her chapter as the respect for multi-racialism, multi-lingualism and multi-religions, which implies seditious attacks on any race, language or religion would not be tolerated; maintenance of law and order; meritocracy, and non-corruption. We have more or less absorbed these fundamental values into our DNA, and so the likelihood is that Singapore will continue to do well. There might be more space for the political opposition and their share of parliamentary seats might increase, but by and large, the dominance of a single party will likely continue.

While I think this first scenario is the most probable, one of the most valuable lessons I learned from my first boss, then Foreign Minister S. Rajaratnam, is to always think the unthinkable. As we now know from the political transitions I cited at the start of this chapter, the unthinkable can happen. So let me address two other possible scenarios for Singapore.

---

[1] The IPS Prism project took place between June 2012 and January 2013 where the Singapore public were invited to discuss their views to the question "How will Singapore govern itself in 2022?" This resulted in scenarios called the IPS Prism Scenarios. For more information, visit the Institute's website: http://www.spp. nus.edu.sg/ips/ipsprism.aspx.

The second scenario is a hard landing. What is a hard landing? If you look all over Asia, there is a pattern of dominant parties staying in power for decades, then getting voted out, and then staging electoral comebacks several years later, like the Indian National Congress, the Liberal Democratic Party in Japan and the Kuomintang in Taiwan. The question now is: can it happen in Singapore too? It is important to ask ourselves what led to these kinds of changes, and how we can prevent them. These transitions generate much uncertainty and inherent risk, that can lead to a weakening of social cohesion and can disrupt economic activity. Incidentally, we should watch very carefully the outcome of the general and state elections that are due in Malaysia, this year. It is very clear that the ruling Barisan Nasional (BN) party knows that these are very important elections. I still believe that BN can win these elections but that seems far from certain. The mere possibility that BN could lose after 40 years in power is a sign of how political change is coming in a fundamental way.

The third scenario is also improbable, but we cannot rule it out because we see it happening in advanced democracies all over the world today. This scenario is political gridlock and paralysis. For example, the United Kingdom (UK) does have a government, but British friends have privately told me that they are horrified at the prospect of a 2017 UK referendum on whether to stay in the European Union as this means five years of enormous uncertainty among investors.[2] Even more strikingly, the world's oldest democracy, the US, as we all know, is also undergoing a remarkable paralysis. Recently, the Harvard economist Kenneth Rogoff published an essay that began:

> "Many foreign observers look at the US budget shenanigans with confusion and dismay, wondering how a country that seems to have it all can manage its fiscal affairs so chaotically. The root problem is not just a hugely elevated level of public debt, or a patently unsustainable trajectory for old age entitlements. It is an electorate deeply divided over the

---

[2] See speech by United Kingdom's Prime Minister, Mr David Cameron, 'EU Speech at Bloomberg', 23 January 2013.

direction of government, with differences compounded by changing demographics and sustained sluggish growth".[3]

If it can happen in the US, how can a small country like Singapore be immune to it?

This discussion is very timely. It is clear from recent events, including the opposition victory in the Punggol East by-election that we are going through a political transition here in Singapore just as the world is going through the same. It is our duty to try and analyse these trends as best we can and prepare for all kinds of futures and, as S. Rajaratnam would have said, to think the unthinkable.

---

[3] Kenneth Rogoff, "World is right to worry about US debt", *Financial Times*, (24 January 2013), http://www.ft.com/intl/cms/s/2/ed300802-63e5-11e2-84d8-00144feab49a.html#axzz2K0IU5luJ.

8

Governing in the Future — Together

LAWRENCE WONG

INTRODUCTION

Over the past few months, I have attended many dialogue sessions and participated in many conversations. In these sessions, I have heard feedback and views on a wide range of policies such as education, healthcare, transport, housing, etc. However, beyond the policy issues, there is a search for something deeper — what Singapore stands for and what it means to be a Singaporean. One person I spoke to felt that Singapore had changed too quickly over the past few years, and that he no longer felt the same sense of connection with the country. Or as another person put it more vividly, "I would like to see a Singapore where buildings are not just commercial premises like shopping centres… I want Singapore to build and promote its traditions from 20 years ago, such as coffee shops (no air-con, please), *mama* shops, Malay barber shops, the old dragon design playgrounds…." So, nearly 50 years after gaining independence, Singapore and Singaporeans are examining "big questions" today: Who are we? What are our values?

These are critical questions as we try to make sense of the changes occurring around us. Life was tougher in the past, but fighting colonial, communist and communal threats, and overcoming deprivation gave older Singaporeans a powerful sense of shared memories and common destiny. There was a strong sense of group solidarity, loyalty to extended families and social cohesion. Today, our environment is becoming more interconnected, complex and uncertain. Advances in technology, the growth of global migration and trade have intensified the pace, intensity and volume of interaction between our people. All this means that the experience of being Singaporean has become more varied. Different Singaporeans will have different priorities: some needing to focus on meeting basic needs; others on wider aspirations; and many, a mix of both.

Ultimately, these issues of identity and social anchors relate back to how we want to govern ourselves. The roles of the government will have to evolve. Among our principles of governance are some enduring ones that continue to be important. After all, we have to deal with the same strategic realities: our geography, history and our multi-religious and multi-racial population have not changed. However, as new challenges arise, fresh principles will emerge, or we will need fresh interpretations of enduring principles.

In this changing environment, all Singaporeans, from the government and businesses, to civil society and individual citizens, must come together to forge a new compact that will allow Singapore to navigate the way forward. Governing in the future will mean casting new roles and relations between the government and citizens, and among citizens themselves, while strengthening and reinforcing values that Singaporeans cherish.

How should our governance principles evolve to address the challenges of the future? Let me share my views in four areas.

MERITOCRACY

First is the issue of meritocracy as a governing principle. This has been the topic of debate recently. I think if you ask most Singaporeans, they would agree that meritocracy has served us well over the years. As a small country, Singapore cannot compete in the world if we do not harness the talents of our people. Moreover, in a multi-ethnic society, any form of discrimination would easily have created resentment and tensions. So ability and performance are a fair and objective basis for making decisions whether it is appointments in the public and private sectors, or admission to our institutions of higher learning.

Having said that, there are concerns that with growing income inequalities, a system of meritocracy would favour those with means. This can undermine social mobility and lead to stratification in society. I understand the concerns. We all have hard-wired in us a deep moral belief and instinct for fairness and just deserts. We agree that people deserve rewards for ability and hard work. So when someone is held back by multiple layers of disadvantage through no fault of his or her own, it upsets our sense of fairness.

Clearly, when taken to extreme, unfettered meritocracy can lead to inequality and a winner-takes-all society. But that does not mean that meritocracy is inherently bad or dysfunctional. More importantly, if we are not going on merit, then how else are we going to determine a person's progression in school or work? I had a chat with several polytechnic students some months back, and they raised concerns about the stress arising from the national Primary School Leaving Examination (PSLE), and how this can be reduced. I asked them if they would prefer a system where progression to the next level was not based on PSLE, but on random balloting. No one wanted such a system. They all still favoured some form of academic assessment, preferably less stressful than the current PSLE, with progression based on merit. So we have to be careful not to throw the baby out with the bathwater.

The challenge for us is to improve our system of meritocracy. We do not want a meritocracy that breeds excessive competition, where people seek primarily to advance their individual interest at the expense of others. We do not want a meritocracy that results in a closed group of winners, where advantages to any individual are ascribed by birth. What we want is to shape a system of meritocracy in Singapore that works for the benefit of all and is consistent with our ideals for a fair and just society.

It is not going to be easy to do this, and there are no ready-made solutions. As Amartya Sen once said, the "idea of meritocracy may have many virtues, but clarity is not one of them." Policy-wise, there are things we can and are doing to keep our system open and mobile. That is why we have already initiated several significant changes in education, for example, by increasing state investments in pre-school so that children get an equal start in life. We will continue to study and review how our policies need to be updated to give full opportunities to every child, especially those who come from disadvantaged homes to fulfil their potential.

At the same time, those who have succeeded must think beyond themselves, and give back to society. They have to show that they care for their fellow citizens, for example, through philanthropy. We see this in the United States (US). People who have become rich are setting up foundations and doing good work. Mayor Michael Bloomberg of New York City was just in the news recently for donating more than US$1 billion to his alma mater Johns Hopkins University. Here too, many Singaporeans are donating generously to good causes. More people should do so according to their means and from their heart. Just as we embrace the value of meritocracy, we should also set new social norms for more giving and philanthropy in Singapore.

It is also important to have a broader and more appropriate concept of meritocracy — one that goes beyond academic success or achievements in a few selected careers. And we are in a better position to do this today than years back because our economy has become more sophisticated thereby creating many more avenues for talents in different areas to be recognised. We already see more and more young Singaporeans pursuing their interests in a diverse range of areas like the arts, fashion, music, sports, etc. We should continue to celebrate talent in these different fields and recognise those who excel, who overcome adversity, who show spirit, character and determination.

MARKETS AND GOVERNMENT

Besides meritocracy, public policy in Singapore has also been guided by a deep appreciation of the critical interdependence between markets and government.

The tension between markets and government is neither new nor unique to Singapore. It has been the central issue in the evolution of political economy and governance models over the last 200 years. The reality is that neither markets nor governments can work effectively on their own. Market principles are needed to help governments work better, and good government is necessary to help markets function more effectively. The balance between markets and government is never static, and has to be re-calibrated continually, according to circumstance and context.

The recent Global Financial Crisis (GFC) and the significant stresses associated with globalisation have put the spotlight on the imperfections and limitations of relying only on the market. I am reminded of what happened in my previous job at the Energy Market Authority (EMA). To manage the risk of our high reliance on imported piped gas from our neighbours, the government decided to import Liquefied Natural Gas

(LNG) to diversify our gas supply sources and enhance our energy security. A private company was appointed to build the LNG terminal, but when the GFC struck in 2007, project financing tightened up, and the project became commercially non-viable. We could have waited till the Crisis passed and allowed for some delays in the project, but we decided that this was important enough to our energy security that it could not be left to the vagaries of the market. So EMA took over the terminal project. We quickly set up a company, assembled a project team virtually from scratch, and with a loan from the Ministry of Finance, got the project started again. Since then, I have been keeping track of the progress of the terminal, and I am glad that in a few months' time, the LNG terminal will be completed, and we will soon be able to import LNG and begin our process of fuel diversification for energy security.

This is a story with a happy ending, of how the government successfully stepped in to address a market failure. And indeed, this is something the government since 1959 has done repeatedly in various sectors — from housing to banking, from the airline industry to military armament. But there are also problems with relying too much on the government.

Take again the example of our power sector, but go further back in time. Many years ago, the power plants and grid used to be owned and operated centrally by the Public Utilities Board (PUB). In government hands, PUB thought that they were doing all they could to be efficient and that they were ready for the functions to be spun off and privatised. But in private hands, the company (Singapore Power) realised that there were still areas for efficiency improvements and for costs to be trimmed. The privatisation and subsequent liberalisation of the electricity market brought more concrete benefits to consumers. Under the heat of market competition, power companies aggressively switched away from the more expensive oil-fired plants to the more cost-efficient natural gas plants. If the power plants had all remained in government hands, this switch to gas would probably have taken a much longer time to materialise and consumers would have been worse off.

So this is the challenge in public policy. The debate is not about nationalisation versus market competition as though they were mutually exclusive options. It is not about government intervening to supplant markets, or allowing market forces to reign unbridled with little or no government oversight. Rather, the real issue is about finding the right balance between markets and government, recognising that both are necessary.

The fact is that in our next phase of development, with slower growth and an ageing population, the state will have to do more and play a more significant role in funding or providing certain core services. The government will make significant investments in pre-school education. We are also doing a lot more to strengthen our social safety nets. In transport, we are making massive investments to expand the rail network and provide more buses. Another area is healthcare, where government spending will double to S$8 billion over the next five years.

As government spending increases, we must ensure that there are sufficient resources to fund and sustain the programmes we want. We can see the mistakes other countries have made — how easy it is for governments to spend beyond their means, and end up with large fiscal burdens and structural deficits. More importantly, state provisions have to be designed so as not to reduce the dignity of individuals, erode work ethic and create dependency on the state. Otherwise, after some time, the economy will stagnate, and the people will suffer.

So what we are striving for is not bigger government, but smarter and better government — one that understands the interdependencies between the state and markets; one that is responsive to the needs of our times, while maintaining the competitive spirit and drive that is so crucial to our existence.

ACTIVE CITIZENS AND STRONG COMMUNITY

The government will do its part to facilitate and lead in terms of the broad policy directions, but it has no monopoly of knowledge or ideas. To understand and tackle our challenges fully and vigorously, we need to draw on the expertise and resources of all our people. This leads me to my next point on the importance of active citizenry, strong communities and vibrant civic society.

Over the years, we have raised the level of engagement between the government and the people, opened up more space for civic groups and alternative views and matured as a society. The growing participation and diversity have been vital pluses for Singapore, enabling us to adapt to changing conditions and to the needs and expectations of a new generation. Going forward in our new environment, I have no doubt that our society will continue to open up. Younger Singaporeans, in particular, would like more space to express themselves, voice diverse views and experiment with new ways of doing things. These are positive trends; they show that Singaporeans care about issues and want to play a part in shaping the future of the country.

Governance must keep pace with these changes in our society. It means more engagement and consultation in policy formulation. It also means more effort on the part of everyone involved to listen to one another, to actively seek out viewpoints that challenge our own assumptions and beliefs, so that we can begin to understand where the people who disagree with us are coming from. Ultimately, we want to discuss issues with reason, passion and conviction; but always in a spirit of respect, so that people with legitimate but bridgeable differences can sit down at the same table and hash things out.

This is why we embarked on the "Our Singapore Conversation" (OSC) process. It is a process for the whole nation to have a conversation about what values are important to us, to engender a sense of rootedness, and to build a stronger consensus on the way forward for Singapore. Such engagement is not new — the government has been engaging Singaporeans in various forms and platforms over the years — but the scale and scope of the engagement are now much wider.

Besides more consultation and engagement on policy issues, we also want to promote active civic participation in solving problems. The late S. Rajaratnam described this as strengthening a democracy of deeds, and not just words. As he put it, we must "encourage participation at all levels to get people away from adversarial democracy to a problem-solving democracy." To facilitate this, the government should pull back from being all things to all citizens, and give Singaporeans the opportunity and space to organise themselves, and develop their own solutions.

Many have observed that when there is a problem, the first question people usually ask is: what will the government do about it? So at a recent OSC meeting, I was struck when a polytechnic student said, "Why must there always be a policy answer to all our problems? Why can't we solve the problems by ourselves?" Over the weekend, I had a conversation with university students, and the theme was "More than ourselves: A generation that cares". These young people reflect the coming of age of a new generation who are more active and engaged, and prepared to do their part for the community. We should encourage more of such civic activism to empower and support Singaporeans to take the initiative and make a difference to the lives of others. This is how we can nurture the *kampung* spirit in our urban city, and strengthen the sense of togetherness in our society.

LEADERSHIP

Finally, let me end on the role of leadership in governance. We have always believed that leadership is key; that as a small country, we need good leaders and able people to serve, whether in the political arena or in public administration.

In a new environment of active citizenry and civic participation, one may be tempted to think that leadership is no longer so important. On the contrary, I believe that leadership remains just as, if not more, critical. But the leadership demands are different. In a complex and rapidly changing environment, knowledge is always localised and fleeting. As a result, leaders are sometimes faced with an "inversion of expertise", where people at the lower levels have more accurate information, and are better able to adapt and respond to changing circumstances. A recent survey by the public relations firm Edelman shows that people tend to put more trust in their peer group, defined as a "person like me", than in traditional "authority" figures. Trust is being expressed in horizontal ways, rather than solely on a vertical axis. So the leadership approach must evolve to one that encourages more open collaboration, feedback and empowerment of our people.

We see this happening in the military. The former US Commander in Afghanistan General Stanley McChrystal once described how he had to adapt to a new leadership style, to operate in a complex, networked environment, and more importantly, to earn the trust and confidence of a younger generation of soldiers. He had to become "a lot more transparent, a lot more willing to listen, a lot more willing to be reverse-mentored from below." Over time, McChrystal said that he came to realise that "leaders aren't good because they are right; they are good because they are willing to learn and to trust."

It sounds easy to do all this, but in fact, leadership in this new environment will be more challenging. It means having the humility to admit that we do not always have all the answers. It means having the courage to take risks and to trust our people to make the right decisions.

With a more diverse population, leaders will have to gather a wide range of suggestions and ideas, and take time to build a consensus. It is not always possible to align everyone to the same view. So leaders also have to decide, explain the basis for the decisions they make, and take responsibility for the outcomes. As short-term populist interests gain increasing voice and traction, leaders must have the moral courage and integrity to retain the long-term perspective, and make the difficult decisions that will yield long-term benefits to Singapore and its citizens.

This ability to look beyond the short term has been crucial to the success of many of our policies. Today, it will be harder to take the long-term view, even as the government's policies and actions are being subjected to daily barracking. The daily incessant round of the 24-hour news cycle, its noise amplified by the social media, will make governance more difficult here as it has elsewhere. This calls for more, not less, leadership. And indeed this is not just a question of political leadership. It is, more fundamentally, about what sort of government we want, and the kind of society we want to be.

CONCLUSION

Meritocracy, the role of the state and markets, active citizenry, and leadership — I have touched on four aspects of governance where I believe our principles have to adapt and change in order to stay relevant in a new environment.

In charting the way forward, we no longer have the benefit of following and adapting best practices by others who are ahead of us. In many ways, we will have to break new ground ourselves and find fresh solutions that are suited to our circumstance and context. Increasingly we will have to experiment, make mistakes, learn from them, and improve ourselves.

More and more is now expected of governments. Some say that it is impossible to meet the high expectations. But almost 50 years ago, the cynics and critics said that a small, resource-scarce country with no hinterland had little chance of survival. In the 1960s and 1970s, some analysts thought in order to survive, a country had to be protectionist and favour domestic production. Singapore proved that we could be exceptional each time; we not only survived but thrived. We eschewed import substitution and found advantages from free trade. The "big questions" of today are the challenge of our generation. We can defy critics and cynics again if we answer these questions together.

CHAPTER 9

Sustaining Good Governance in an Era of Rapid and Disruptive Change

DONALD LOW

HOW IS OUR CONTEXT CHANGING?

The main issue that I want to address is how we can sustain good governance in an era of rapid and disruptive change. I believe that more so than before, Singapore will face greater volatility, uncertainty and complexity.

We have seen this economically: we experienced more shocks to our economy in the last 15 years than in the 30 years before that. Much of this is due to our growing connectedness with the global economy, to hyper-globalisation and unfettered capital flows, as well as rapid technological change that is shortening business cycles.

Politically, the government's space for manoeuvre has also narrowed. Its traditionally admired solutions in a number of areas — housing, healthcare, education, transport and infrastructure — have come under greater scrutiny and debate. This partly reflects a more contested political scene, but it also suggests that policy-making has become more complex, and the trade-offs, sharper and starker.

These economic and political trends will interact with social forces such as the ageing of our population, rising inequality, wage stagnation, lower social mobility and a larger foreign population to create new stressors on social cohesion.

Citizens' trust in the government's ability to deliver can no longer be assumed. The pristine "policy lab" in which our policy-makers used to operate is being replaced by a more critical public, and by a more diverse polity with competing interests. Increasingly, our policy-makers have to make *hard choices* — where there are winners and losers — not just remind themselves of hard truths in government. Citizens are directly impacted by the stark choices that the government makes, but their expectations of the government and the outcomes they seek may not always match what the latter can realistically deliver.

Sustaining good governance in this new, more complex and uncertain environment is not impossible, but it would require significant institutional and policy reforms on the part of the government.

THE RESILIENCE IMPERATIVE

In an era of rapid and disruptive change, the most valuable asset a government can have is resilience. Resilience is the capacity of a system to bounce back, not necessarily to its original form, but to one that allows the system to maintain its core purpose and integrity, and to continue performing its main functions.

Resilience — whether of an ecological system, an organisation, or a species — is usually a function of two things. First, a resilient system is one that has been exposed to a *variety* of shocks. Each of these shocks is not large enough to destroy the system but, over time, they force the system to adapt and to develop capabilities to respond to a wider range of shocks and stimuli. Conversely, systems that are fragile are those that have been insulated from external shocks or protected from competition. This is why the Galapagos Islands are ecologically so fragile, even if they are stable and seemingly sustainable.

We also saw in the Global Financial Crisis (GFC) of 2007–2009 how a lack of variety created a highly fragile financial system. The health of banks became tightly coupled to the availability of cheap credit, rising house prices and the willingness of home owners to continually re-finance their mortgages. Financial institutions mostly pursued a strategy of originating and then securitising sub-prime mortgages. The result was that there was too much mimicry and insufficient variety in the financial system. Such systems built on a monoculture can exhibit long periods of stability, but are also extremely vulnerable to the slightest shock. The collapse of Lehman Brothers had such far-reaching and catastrophic consequences, not because it was a particularly large investment bank, but because it was highly connected in the financial system in the United States (US). And because many other institutions were doing the same thing, there was a great deal of "interlocking fragility" such that when Lehman collapsed, the entire banking system became vulnerable too.

The second essential ingredient of a resilient system is *selection*. Resilient systems all have some mechanism for "choosing" between competing strategies and designs. We normally think of the selection process as being undertaken by individuals or leaders. Yet we can also think of selection that is constantly being undertaken by impersonal forces such as the market. Markets are resilient because they encourage variety and diversity, and because they are a highly effective way of selecting "fit" strategies or designs, and then replicating and scaling them up. As the economist William Baumol points out, markets are "innovation machines".

This resilience perspective, which I have used to describe both ecological and economic systems, can also be applied to the study of governance systems. If we agree that what governance needs most in the context of rapid and disruptive change is resilience, then we would also agree it needs to foster diversity and variety as well as competitive selection processes that are not reliant on a few individuals making the right calls.

While it is extremely tempting for the human mind to respond to more shocks with a desire for control, harmony and stability, the reality is that the avoidance of shocks and failures is a utopian dream. More problematically, insulation from competition and shocks breeds brittleness and fragility.

A political system can also suffer from too much mimicry and have too little variety to allow for the experimentation and adaptation that is needed for long-term survival. Without sufficient variety, a political system can become trapped by groupthink and ideological rigidity. The psychologist Irving Janis coined the term "groupthink" to explain poor decision-making by groups. Its key signs are a strong illusion of invulnerability by decision-makers, a belief in the inherent morality of the group, the stereotyping of those who do not agree with the group's perspective, and simplistic moral formulations that discourage deeper, rational analysis. Self-appointed guardians of the dominant ideology prevent alternative views from being aired and place significant pressure on dissenters, creating an illusion of unanimity, even if dissent is rampant below the surface.

I believe that this resilience perspective ought to replace the vulnerability narrative on which the government frequently relies. Rather than emphasise our vulnerability and how this imposes all sorts of constraints on what Singapore can do or can be, resilience thinking frames the discussion on governance expansively. It invites us to think about what institutional shock absorbers we need in a more volatile world, how we can achieve a better allocation of risks between the state and citizens, and how we should secure Singaporeans' confidence for the future.

BETTER INSTITUTIONS

Having identified resilience as the central imperative for our political system, let me suggest two areas of reforms that a resilience perspective in governance entails. The first is that we need better institutions, rules and norms to safeguard good governance in Singapore; the second is reforming meritocracy.

First, better institutions, rules and norms. For those who are familiar with the principles of governance that are taught in schools, there are four of such principles.[1] The first of these is "leadership is key". The elaboration of this principle is that given our inherent vulnerabilities, Singapore needs leaders of great ability and high integrity, individuals who will do "what is right, not what is popular." I think most Singaporeans will agree that effective and far-sighted leadership is essential for Singapore.

But if we apply a resilience lens, as opposed to just a vulnerability perspective, then we are likely to say that while leadership matters, good institutions matter too and possibly more so in the long run. This is partly because leadership is highly dependent on context. Good leaders in one context may make for terrible ones in another. Churchill was a great wartime prime minister, but he was far less effective in peacetime.

More importantly, the principle of "leadership is key" goes against the grain of the argument here that what determines resilience is not a wise man or a group of elites knowing the right answers. Rather, it is by ensuring

---

[1] The other three principles are: Reward for work, work for reward (or meritocracy); opportunities for all, a stake for everyone and anticipate change, stay relevant.

sufficient variety and diversity in the system that we increase resilience. In the long run, we are better off relying on system of distributed intelligence — on Singapore having a diversity of ideas and competing options, than on a system that is critically dependent on a small group of bright people.

So beyond the "leadership is key" principle, I would like to see a principle around the importance of having institutions that support dissent, variety, experimentation and selection. Translating this into practice would see the government give citizens and researchers more access to information, and support social science research as much as it does the hard sciences. Greater disclosure of information that is jealously guarded by public agencies and greater transparency of government's decision-making processes bolster trust in our system of governance and enhance government's credibility. Encouraging greater variety may also mean instituting the practice of red teams versus blue teams across government to encourage a healthy contest of ideas. Because the executive branch in the government has been a highly successful one, and one that has been relatively insulated from competition, the risks of insufficient variety and of inadequate pressures for it to adapt are quite real. It therefore has to make a special effort to create mechanisms that would foster greater variety and selection in the system.

Leaders of the governing People's Action Party have, in the recent past, expressed their concern about how increasing political polarisation might paralyse government. The greater worry should be about how the human desire for control, harmony and stability, might weaken the already weak incentives for policy-makers to allow competing ideas to surface, and to subject these to serious debate and analysis. In short, the risks of polarisation are less worrisome than the risks arising from the numbing effects of incumbency, the inertia of the status quo and the tyranny of old ideas for Singapore.

REFORMING MERITOCRACY

Second, meritocracy. This is a principle of governance that we hold dear, the practice of which should be tempered and reformed if we adopt a resilience perspective. The idea of meritocracy is that rewards should be allocated on the basis of a person's talents and abilities. But an equally critical question that we should ask is what *rules* should constrain the behaviour of those who have done well in the meritocratic system. There is no *prima facie* reason to believe that those who have succeeded in a meritocracy will channel their energies to improving society's well-being.

Indeed, as the GFC has shown, it is possible that those who have succeeded in a meritocracy may engage in morally hazardous activities and demand government bailouts when the risks they have taken go bad.

The kind of meritocracy that was practised on Wall Street also breeds a self-justifying, entitlement narrative. Wall Street bankers justified the decision to pay themselves millions in bonuses from bailout monies on the grounds that not doing so would cause talent to leave the financial industry. This kind of meritocracy breeds a belief among its beneficiaries that they are entitled to their rewards, that the market system is inherently just and that inequality is natural. They view those who have not succeeded in the system as slothful or lacking in merit and thus undeserving of state support. Such a system increases resistance by the rich to the redistributive policies needed to address inequality. Over time, it entrenches inequality and immobility, and society becomes more stratified and divided by class.

Singaporeans are often reminded of the risks and moral hazards of providing more help for the poor. This is the main justification as to why we must not have a welfare state. The GFC is a reminder that the risks of moral hazards are far greater when the rich are not properly regulated and reined in. Corporate malfeasance imposes much larger costs on society than the often-cited entitlement mentality of the poor who are addicted to government welfare.

So to conclude, I would very much like to see the principle of meritocracy augmented by a principle that emphasises fairness and social justice. Translating this into practice means avoiding conflicts of interest; ensuring the independence of public institutions; having strong safeguards against regulatory capture; and increasing transparency and public accountability. It also means strengthening our social safety nets and other redistributive institutions as well as ensuring a fairer allocation of risks between state and citizens, between rich and poor.

10

The Emergent in Governance in Singapore

GILLIAN KOH

The party that has governed Singapore since 1959, the People's Action Party (PAP), has had to face bruising political contests in the General Election of May 2011, where it suffered a 6.5% decline in its vote share vis-à-vis its political opposition. In two subsequent by-elections in May 2012 and January 2013, it lost to the candidates of the main opposition party, the Workers' Party.

These developments reflect a mood on the ground that people want change — change in the way the government relates to them and by which it designs its public policies; change in the way that citizens want life and society ordered. Also, diverse views about what those changes should be have emerged. Other chapters in this volume have addressed the different ways in which the model is beginning to change to respond to these trends. This chapter provides survey material to indicate what the ground expects. It ends by suggesting that the same political trend was witnessed in the other developmental states in East Asia, resulting in a higher level of political activism and expanding scope in social support by the state in them.

TREND-SPOTTING

There is, if we may borrow a term from the economists, a "secular trend" towards a greater level of political pluralism among Singaporeans. It is most likely the result of a growing sense of political competency as more Singaporeans are better educated and have become affluent, as referred to in Chapter 1 by Professor Chan Heng Chee. It is also reinforced by the transition of the younger generations of Singaporeans into the voting public, those who did not participate or witness the early battles of statehood. Products of a more secure society, they expect political parties to establish a connection with them, directly and in a way that respects their freedom of choice. They do not want their support to be taken for granted. Finally, with Singapore being an open, highly globalised city-state, the benefits of development have had a different impact on different people. While the state has made on-going efforts to redistribute the benefits of economic growth with more subsidies and social support, especially to the needy and low-income, these have been deemed inadequate, raising a sense of social injustice as the differences in incomes and lifestyles between those at the working class and the professional and entrepreneurial classes have widened. These are some of the social bases for the diversity in political interests and attitudes that have arisen.

Two surveys of attitudes about the general elections conducted by the Institute of Policy Studies provide support for the analysis above. The Post-Election Surveys of 2006 and 2011 indicated that the desire for political pluralism rose among the higher occupational classes, the more affluent and those who are better educated. The desire for political pluralism is also higher among the younger voters and possibly more so with each set of younger voters. The conclusions will be more robust with after we collect more data points, but for now the electoral results, the political discourse and these two sets of data can inform us about the changing relationship between citizens and the PAP, and their role in the governance system. Reported by Yahoo! News on 8 February 2013, a poll conducted by Blackbox Research of Punggol East voters after the by-election showed that while issues on cost of living were important to 39% of respondents, 17% said the government was not listening to them, of which one-fifth were below 40 years of age. Another 7% said they were guided by the need for stronger opposition to the PAP in parliament in their voting preference, and emphasised the role of a political opposition as integral to governance.

THE IPS PRISM PROJECT

In 2011, the Institute embarked on a year-long project called IPS Prism to better understand the trends in political attitudes among Singaporeans and seek out "the emergent" in governance, from the ground. The project was designed as a scenario planning process centred on the question: How will Singapore govern itself in 2022? Assuming two regular five-year parliamentary terms, the time horizon in the project would be two election cycles from the time the project was conducted. In the first of two stages of the study, 140 people closely associated with seven key sectors of society were asked to develop scenarios showing the possible trajectories that governance in Singapore might take from then till 2022. In the second stage, one set of scenarios from the first stage was presented with members of the public who were then invited to share their own thoughts about how Singapore would or should be governed. In this way, we were able to get a sense of what meanings people attached to governance; what concerned them and what their hopes were. This was collected in the IPS Prism Survey and constituted the third phase of the project. Its findings are discussed later in this chapter.

In the first stage, the top three trends that participants felt had the potential to shape governance significantly over the next decade, yet were the most uncertain in how they would play out exactly were first, the sense of trust and credibility that the government of the day enjoyed from the public — did they believe that the government served them and knew how best to serve them effectively? The second was how society defined success — by material standards or by non-material moral values. Third was how the social compact between government and people was designed — would it be one tailored to provide greater support to those with the most potential and rewards for the high achievers because of the benefits they bring to the rest of society, or a system that provided a more egalitarian system of distributing support and rewards?

Key concerns for the select group in this first stage of the project were the value system of Singaporean society, national identity and threats to social cohesion like income distribution, and trust in the government. In a democratic process, the participants voted on scenarios that they felt would be most plausible and yet challenging. There were 40 sets of scenarios that were developed in the first stage of the process. The set that received the highest votes in the final workshop, built on the three trends described above, were as follows:

SingaStore — a pro-business, high-growth world that the public trusts, which invests in people and endeavours that have the highest potential to create economic value. The question was how socially sustainable it would be.

SingaGives — a pro-Singaporean scenario where the public trusts a new government and elected president to implement an egalitarian policy framework that is supported through the use of the national reserves. The question was how fiscally sustainable it would be.

WikiCity — a pro-active scenario where a new coalition government is elected to trim the role of the state because of citizens' low trust in government, which allows for self-organising communities to emerge and meet the daily needs of the people. The question was how politically sustainable it would be.

These are the IPS Prism Scenarios.

THE IPS PRISM SURVEY

In the second stage, the IPS Prism Scenarios were brought to life in an immersive arts experience. Members of the public were invited to participate in creating exhibits and forum theatre designed around the trends and scenarios. They were brought through the IPS stories of governance in 2022, and then invited to share their own stories of "life in 2022". Using a method called "Narrative Capture" (developed by a company called Cognitive Edge), people who attended the immersive arts experience[1] or watched the material that was recorded and placed at an IPS Prism website were invited to volunteer their stories about what they thought their life would be like in 2022. They then answered a set of questions in what is called "tagging", which allowed researchers to find out more about the respondents' stories. There was a second set of questions that asked participants for their opinions on other issues related to their values and governance.

---

[1] The immersive arts experience was held at the National Library Building between 8 and 15 November 2012.

A total of 600 participants volunteered to complete the IPS Prism Survey. This was not designed as a representative sample of Singaporeans as it only surveyed people who attended the immersive arts experience or people who found out about it on the Internet. The profile of the respondents is as follows: 71.2% respondents were between the ages of 21 and 39, so they were primarily in the younger working ages; 81% lived in four-room, five-room and executive flats and private property, so the relatively affluent were over-represented in this sample; 81.2% were Chinese and 50% of them had no dependents; and 89% were citizens. This profile fits the younger, more affluent profile of voters who were likely to be inclined to support political pluralism, as shown in the earlier general election surveys.

What is good governance?

In the first set of findings, we pulled together views about the "goal of governance". When asked how they would judge the government, there was a bias towards assessing it by whether it "improves the well-being of people", with some saying that it depended also on whether it "delivers economic growth", or "gives people the freedom to do what they want".

This result can be read from the diagram below, called "Triad 1". The dots indicate how respondents "signified" the story that they had submitted about "life in 2022" earlier in the survey. They were asked to place themselves in a way that indicated how they would judge the government in their story, or the sentiment behind their story.[2] Most of the responses were related in some way to governance that "improves the well-being of people". We clustered the responses by the patterns as indicated below.

The overall consensus is that attending to well-being rather than just achieving economic growth is what "good governance" should be about.
In another set of triads, respondents were asked for their opinions rather than to signify their stories. In "Opinion Triad 4", in relation to the "goal of governance", respondents were asked how they would like governance to be guided. The diagram "Opinion A4" shows that they were more likely to say

---

[2] Each dot in a triad diagram indicates where a respondent placed himself or herself to "signify" his or her story, or where he or she stands in the case of an "opinion triad".

that they want Singapore to be governed by "moral values" rather than "economic goals" and "common sense".

Triad 1: I would judge the government by whether it:

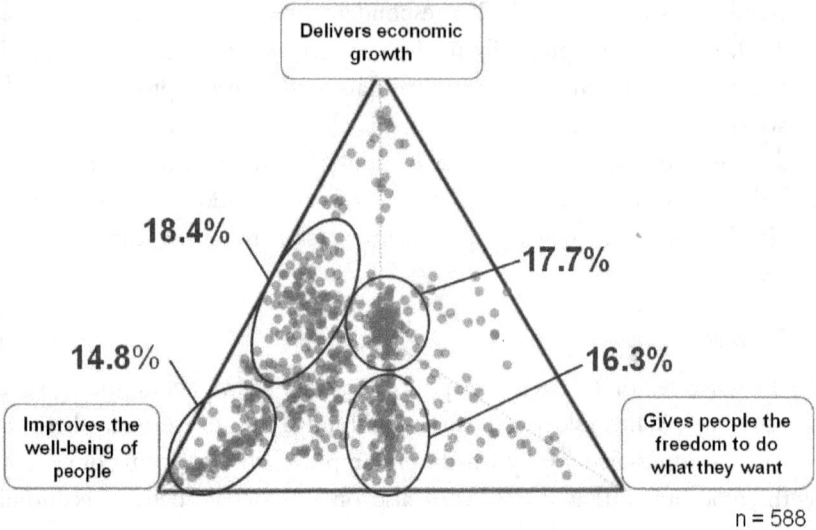

n = 588

Opinion Triad A4:
In 2022, I would like Singapore to be governed by:

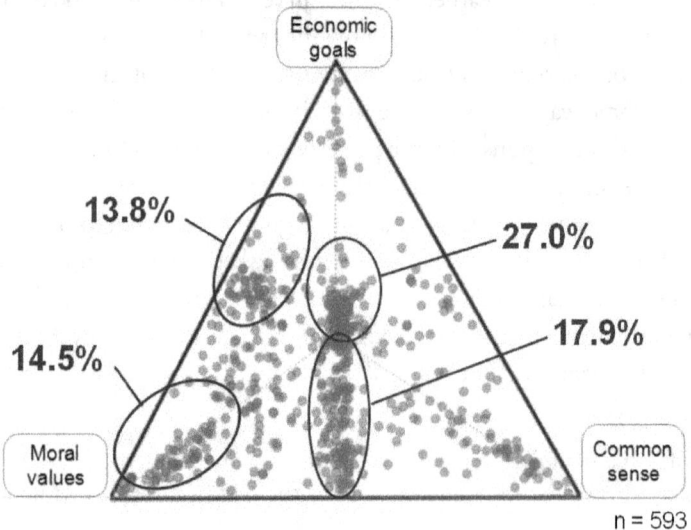

n = 593

The result suggests that for this set of respondents, the performance legitimacy of the PAP government, that used to be based primarily on economic achievement, has run its course. Trust in government for this group would depend on its moral direction and ability to address the higher order goal of "well-being".

Who provides what and to whom?

The second set of findings has to do with who should provide basic goods like housing, healthcare, education and transportation, and to whom. As we find, in the diagram "Triad 2", the bias in responses was towards provision by the government with some role for the community. A quarter of the respondents, however, did indicate that these basic goods should be provided by the government, community as well as business sector. When asked which group should be given priority in receiving help from the government, respondents tended to think that it was the needy rather than "everyone equally" and certainly not "the people who can contribute the most to society". This can be seen in the diagram "Triad 3".

Triad 2: The main provider of what I need (healthcare, education, housing and transportation) should be:

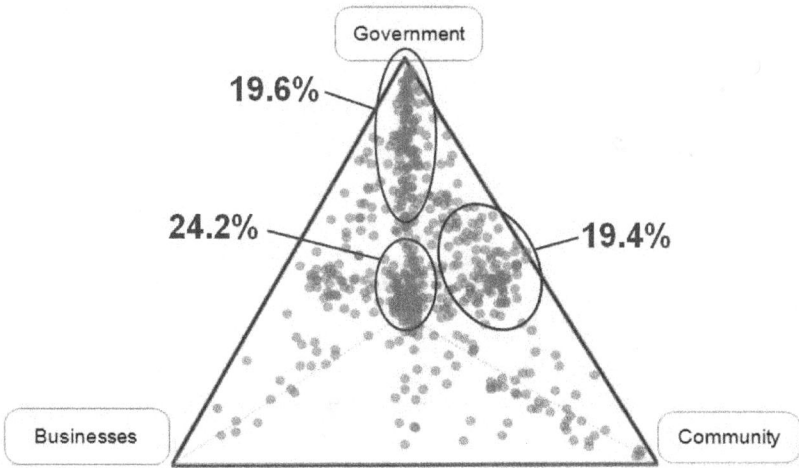

n = 583

Triad 3: The first to receive support from the government should be:

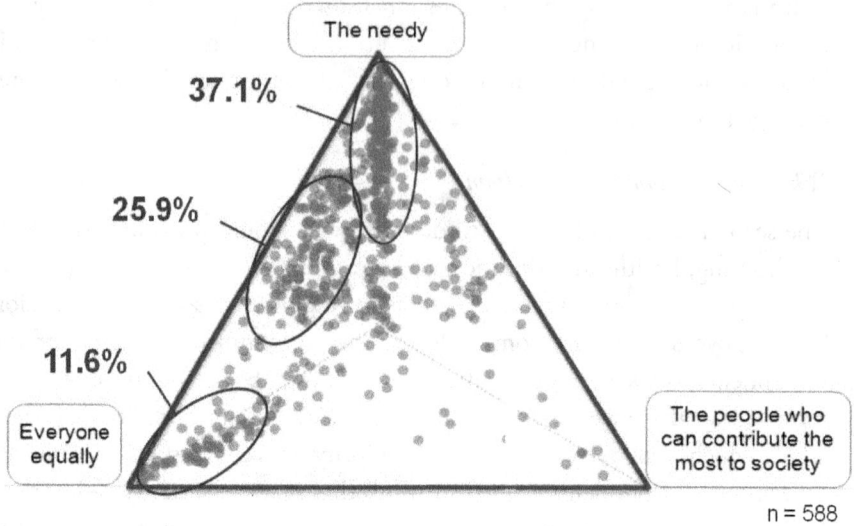

37.1%

25.9%

11.6%

The needy

Everyone equally

The people who can contribute the most to society

n = 588

Triad 4: The government should help these people first:

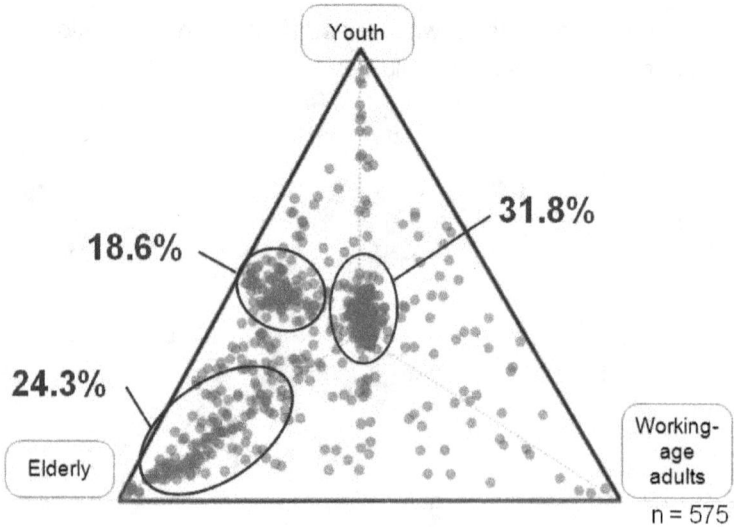

Youth

18.6%

31.8%

24.3%

Elderly

Working-age adults

n = 575

When they were asked which demographic group — the youth, the elderly and working-age adults — should be the first to receive help, respondents were more likely to be biased towards helping the elderly, as shown in the diagram "Triad 4". It should be noted that as many as 31.8% said that the help should go equally to all three groups.

What is the role of the government? How should it provide its support?

The third set of findings has to do with views on how the government should then do its part in meeting basic needs. As seen in the diagram "Triad 5", respondents were likely to say that the government should help people in a way that encourages independence and allows them to "help themselves", through partial subsidies of the costs of basic needs. Thus, for IPS Prism participants, big government would still be in fashion in 2022, and its support would be targeted specifically at the needy, the elderly, with the guiding principle of empowering citizens and subsidising basic costs of living. It is not, however, a typical form of egalitarianism where support is given to all as equally as possible.

Triad 5: The government should:

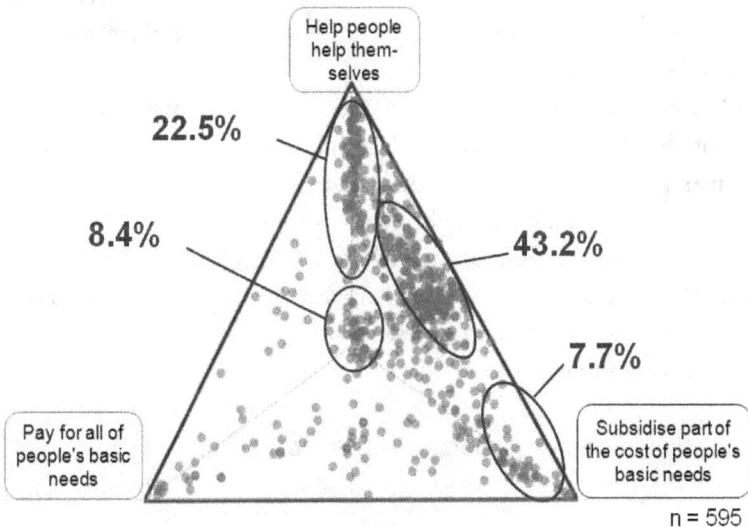

Help people help them- selves

22.5%

8.4%

43.2%

7.7%

Pay for all of people's basic needs

Subsidise part of the cost of people's basic needs

n = 595

Leadership and the Concept of the Vote

As a follow-up to the issues of governance, the survey also asked respondents to signify their story in terms of where and how "leadership" in Singapore would arise from and how it should be exercised. This time there were only two poles of opinions. In Polarity 1, the majority of the respondents felt that the government in 2022 was likely to "support new ideas regardless of the past", while a minority expressed that their notion of the government in 2022 would be "rooted in tradition, ignoring new ideas".

Polarity 1: In my story, the government

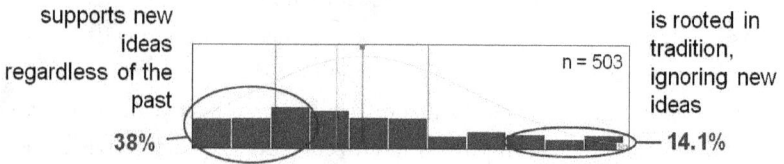

supports new ideas regardless of the past 38% ——— n = 503 ——— is rooted in tradition, ignoring new ideas 14.1%

Also, a majority of the respondents were likely to say in their stories that leadership in 2022 should arise from the community or a mix of the community and government. This is certainly a shift from the situation where most would accept that Singapore has benefitted from leadership that has stemmed from an active and assertive state sector since the country's independence, see Polarity 2.

Finally, respondents were asked their opinions about the concept or value of the vote in an opinion triad. In Opinion Triad A3, many of the responses were clustered around the idea that the vote "ensures many voices are heard", where 25.5% thought that this should be married with the idea of the vote being "a check on power", and 24.2% thought the vote should "be a check on power" as well as "provide the power to rule". For these respondents, the issue of fair representation of interests and concerns across society was an important ideal.

Polarity 2: In my story, leadership should be:

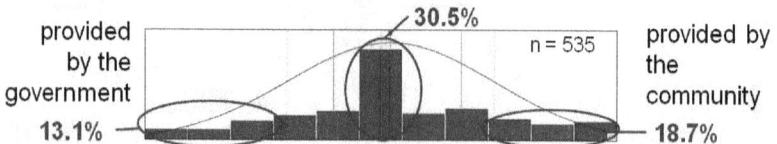

provided by the government 13.1% ——— 30.5% ——— n = 535 ——— provided by the community 18.7%

84

Opinion Triad A3:
It's most important to me that my vote is used to:

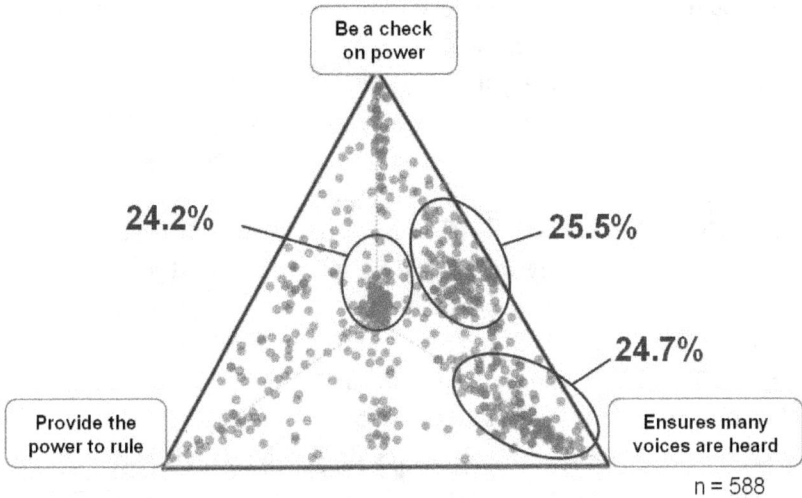

Be a check
on power

24.2%

25.5%

24.7%

Provide the
power to rule

Ensures many
voices are heard

n = 588

CONCLUSION

Once again, while the findings do not reflect the opinions of all Singaporeans, given how the project is designed to look for "the emergent", an over-representation of the young seems appropriate to the task. While the expectation was that the state should provide for basic needs, with a great deal of consideration for the needs of the seniors given that we are an ageing society, the clear signal is that people of the IPS Prism Survey were post-material in their concern for well-being and liberal in their concern that the political system provides a good representation of interests across society. It is not the case that the material was unimportant, but that they aimed for the higher order goal of well-being.

They provide a context for the concerns about income distribution, the government's labour policy and economic strategy. There has been the worry that economic growth is being achieved by all-too-liberal strategy of allow foreign labour into the country. The argument is that wages are depressed at the bottom end of the labour market from large supply of foreign workers, and Singaporeans are crowded out from middle-management jobs (again from comparatively cheaper white collar foreign workers). There is also concern that Singaporeans are being crowded out culturally and that the city-state is congested with more people than its infrastructure can sustain. On this one policy point alone, it is possible to understand why citizens wish that the government would reach beyond just the question of economic growth.

The situation in Singapore is not all too different from the political developments in other East Asian countries like South Korea and Taiwan. Long after their democratic transitions from authoritarian regimes and economic transformation from state-directed capitalism, the progression to more diverse and unequal societies has led the respective populations to wish for participatory governance and greater state-funded social support to give people the assurance that their needs will be met. These political demands have been exacerbated by the uncertainty that has arisen with the ups and downs of the global economy since the turn of the millennium. Politicians and policy-makers in Singapore thus join their counterparts in developed East Asia in their search for progressive social policies to prove that the governance regime is a responsive one and deserves the trust of its people.

11

The Role of Political Competition in Promoting Well-being

SYLVIA LIM

Last week, the Institute of Policy Studies forwarded me a copy of the report on the IPS Prism Survey for my information. One interesting finding I came across was how Singaporeans judge government performance. The survey respondents were asked to choose among three deliverables that the government could focus on — economic growth, giving citizens the freedom to do what they want, or improving the well-being of the people. Many of the respondents indicated that improving the well-being of the people should be the paramount task of the government.

This view that economic growth should not be the end game for governments is in line with trends in other countries. Economists have also written about the side effects of high growth — called the Paradox of High Growth — that tend to bring about higher inequalities and other social problems. There has been a moving away from Gross Domestic Product (GDP) measures as the key indicators of progress; in 2008, Nobel Laureate economist Joseph Stiglitz was asked by the French President Nicolas Sarkozy to come up with a better measure of social progress for France, while Bhutan's Gross National Happiness index is gaining traction internationally.

Sometimes this happiness index is misunderstood. It is not about emotions per se. Measures such as sustainable development, environmental conservation and good governance are key concepts. In July 2011, the UN General Assembly adopted a resolution entitled "Happiness towards a holistic approach to development" that was co-sponsored by 66 countries including Singapore. This resolution stated in its preamble that "the gross domestic product indicator, by nature, was not designed to and does not adequately reflect the happiness and well-being of people in a country." Member countries were then invited to "pursue the elaborations of additional measures that better capture the importance of the pursuit of happiness and well-being in development with a view to guiding their public policies." Since Singapore co-sponsored the resolution, we can assume the government accepts improving Singaporeans' well-being as a key goal. How does this affect policy-making? The devil is always in the details.

Life in Singapore has changed a lot over a short period of time, leaving many Singaporeans with a sense of insecurity and lack of a sense of place in the country. Urban renewal has wiped out most of our childhood memories. Singapore has also become a very unequal society. There was a recent study of world economies by Knight Frank and Citi Private Bank. According to their *Wealth Report 2012*, Singapore was listed as the world's most affluent country with a GDP per capita of about S$70,000 in 2010, beating Norway and the United States. It was stated that Singapore had the highest GDP per capita in 2010, and will likely remain at the top spot as far as 2050. This macro-statistic does not mean much on the ground, where people worry about healthcare costs, housing prices and competition from foreigners in the workplace. The need for stronger safety nets and protection looms large.

So what is the role of politicians and political parties in promoting well-being? The governing party's role is clear, since it is in the position of initiating policies and implementing them. But what about other parties such as the Workers' Party (WP)?

Our belief is that political competition is a safeguard to improve Singaporeans' lives. We provide competition at elections, requiring the government to convince voters that it is performing its role well. Outside of election time, it is also our responsibility to promote good governance.

In this light, having elected opposition members of parliament is important in several ways. First, we assist residents in direct dealings with government departments, and can see first-hand the effects and side effects of policies. Second, we run the local town councils, and can look in detail at the issues relating to town management which affect the quality of life of Singaporeans. On the other hand, the public also holds us accountable for our town management, which is a good thing as well. Third, we can keep the government accountable on matters of public interest by pressing for answers in Parliament, with the protection of Parliamentary privilege.

As political parties, we need to constantly check ourselves against getting too embroiled in partisan politics to miss the wood for the trees. The wood here is the people's well-being, which should always be the guiding light in our actions. We should guard against excessive one-upmanship and ask ourselves: where does the greater good lie? With this in mind, I have personally made it a point to make submissions to the government in certain policy areas that I am familiar with, ahead of any public debate. This is to enable the relevant ministry to consider my views fully and carefully. My experience shows that the ministries were objective and even took my views on board to revise proposed legislation.

Going forward, WP will continue to assist the government when we can and when it is appropriate. While political parties may fight electoral battles, I think it is possible to operate in a culture of mutual respect and give-and-take; it is possible for different political parties to co-exist in this ecosystem for the benefit of all and for the survival of Singapore.

CHAPTER 12

Consensus Rather than Contest will Secure Singapore's Future

KISHORE MAHBUBANI AND
CHUA BENG HUAT

*For Singapore Perspectives 2014, a new element was added to the conference —
that of a debate that included audience polling. The debate motion was, "This
conference resolves that consensus rather than contest will secure Singapore's
future". The proposer was Professor Kishore Mahbubani, Dean of the Lee Kuan
Yew School of Public Policy, National University of Singapore, while the opposer
was Professor Chua Beng Huat from the Department of Sociology, Faculty of
Arts and Social Sciences, National University of Singapore. Three rounds of
polling were conducted — before, during and after the debate. The debate
was chaired by Ms Debra Soon, Managing Director, Channel NewsAsia,
MediaCorp Pte Ltd.*

Emcee: The afternoon programme for Singapore Perspectives 2014 [is] a
face-off between two leading intellectuals in Singapore. They will debate the
motion "This conference resolves that consensus rather than contest will
secure Singapore's future". The proposer is Professor Kishore Mahbubani, an
academic, diplomat and frequently-published expert on Asian and world
affairs. Professor Mahbubani is Dean of the Lee Kuan Yew School of Public
Policy at the National University of Singapore. In 2010 and 2011, he was
selected as one of the top 100 global thinkers by *Foreign Policy*, a magazine on

global politics, economics and ideas. Opposing the motion is Professor Chua Beng Huat, a renowned sociologist and a commentator on comparative politics in Southeast Asia, urban planning and public housing, and rising consumerism. He has contributed to the shaping of young minds in Singapore for over two decades as a professor at the National University of Singapore.

During the course of the debate, we will be inviting [you,] the audience, to use your polling devices to register your agreement with either the proposer, the Dean, or the opposer, Professor Chua. This will be done a number of times so we can see if your view changes as the debate progresses. And we are delighted to have a familiar face from the Singapore media chairing the debate today. She is someone you would have seen on television news, Ms Debra Soon, currently Managing Director of Channel NewsAsia, MediaCorp Pte Ltd. I will now hand over to Ms Soon to tell you more about the rules of this debate.

Chairperson: Thank you very much. Indeed it is a privilege and honour to be here today to chair this illustrious panel together with this illustrious crowd. Professor Mahbubani and Professor Chua both need no introduction even though Lynn has done an excellent job. I think that IPS has been particularly brilliant in coming up with this debate format, and I do expect an extremely entertaining and engaging session – firstly, because neither of them got to choose the topic that they are speaking on. It was assigned. The debate format will also allow them, in the competitive nature of this contest, to do their best to win the argument, to persuade and challenge with the most provocative and interesting ideas, without having to worry that they will be labelled as personally believing in those ideas.

The motion [is]: "This conference resolves that consensus rather than contest will secure Singapore's future". We will have eight minutes at the start with the proposer, eight minutes for the opposer. After that, we will have one question to each of them and they will cross-examine each other. We will take a vote again and after that, we will open the floor to questions. Alright, so at the start now, I am supposed to ask all of you to take your position and vote for whether you agree with the motion that "This conference resolves that consensus rather than contest will secure Singapore's future", and we will see whether or not your views change along the way. Your poll questions start now. So if you agree, please press "1" and if you do not agree please press "2".

1ST VOTING RESULT:
PROPOSITION — 274, OPPOSITION — 187

Chairperson: Very interesting. Kishore, you do not have to pull the bull up the hill. Without further ado, I would like to invite the proposer of the motion, Professor Kishore, to state his position and give us his opening remarks.

Proposer: Thank you Debra. As you said, the vote was a big surprise. I thought the IPS crowd would be in favour of contestation, not consensus. I think we chose the wrong crowd. It was also a mistake to ask an argumentative Indian like me, to support consensus, when in fact it should be a consensual Chinese, like Beng Huat, who should be supporting consensus. But I do actually, fortunately, believe that at this stage of Singapore's development, we do need more consensus than contestation. Because I think that if you really want to discuss the issue of consensus versus contestation, you have to add another "C" word, and the other "C" word is "context". There may have been a time, maybe 10 or 20 years ago, when we would probably have been better off having more contestation, but in today's context, it is very clear that we are entering a completely new political era in Singapore. Of course, with the benefit of hindsight, we can see clearly that for about 40 years from, let us say, 1971 to 2011, Singapore essentially lived in a wonderful political bubble. I begin with 1971 because then, we had made sufficient progress after independence, and I end with 2011 because the 2011 election, as you all know, was a watershed election.

In those 40 years, we had year after year, decade after decade of continuing peace and prosperity. And we came to take it for granted that this is the normal situation for Singapore. But what I am going to suggest is that the last 40 years have actually been very abnormal, and that the normal is actually coming back to Singapore. And when the normal comes back to Singapore, that is when you begin to realise that, yes, we need more consensus than contestation. How would I categorise this new normal? Well, the best way to describe what is normal is to look at other countries — to understand what is normal for most countries in the world. If you look around at the world since the post-independence era, virtually no country like Singapore has gone from Third World to First in one generation. And just that sheer fact makes us so exceptional, and it also makes it very clear that we have not been a normal country.

So let me give you some examples of normal countries and what Singapore might have to deal with as we return to the norm. Firstly, when the British started the decolonisation process — and we all know that the British Empire extended all over the world — they left behind multiracial British colonies everywhere. To mention a few: Guyana in South America, Cyprus in Europe, Sri Lanka in South Asia, Singapore in Southeast Asia, and Fiji in the Pacific. And if you look at these five examples, four out of the five have experienced turmoil, and in some cases, like Sri Lanka and Cyprus, very painful wars and divisions. By contrast, Singapore, since 1969, has experienced complete peace and harmony.

So is the peace and harmony that we enjoyed in the last 40 years the norm, or is what was experienced by the other ex-British multiracial colonies the norm? I suggest to you that as we move towards the norm, there will be rising divisions in Singapore. And this will happen even if we do the right things internally, because some of the challenges are going to seep into Singapore from outside. This morning, an audience[1] said – and I must say, he was very brave in saying so – that Singaporeans do not understand the Malays and the Muslims, and in many ways they do not understand because it is forces that come from outside which influence the Malay-Muslim community.

Let me give you a simple example of the transformation. When I went to Kuala Lumpur as a student to visit the University of Malaya campus in 1969, I saw young Malay girls wearing miniskirts in the 1960s like everyone else. Today, I go back to the same campus, I don't see any Malay girls wearing any miniskirts, and 99.9% dress with a *tudung*. What happened? Was it an internal transformation, or was it an external transformation? It was external. This does not mean that what they did was wrong, but they have changed. Have we understood the change? I can tell you that for a primarily Chinese

---

[1] An audience asked a question in the first session about how well Malays were understood by Singaporeans.

majority society, at a time when the number one emerging power in the world is China, and at a time when China's influence will grow, in every sense, politically, culturally, economically, if you are going to say that the Singapore Chinese community will not be affected by this at all, that its primary identity will always be Singaporean, it is conceivable. But you all know, if you look around the world, more and more societies are being influenced by external trends, and paradoxically, since we have chosen as our destiny to be the most open, the most globalised city in the world, guess what? We will be the most open to all these new global ways. And when they come, you will all say, please let us have more consensus in Singapore. Thank you.

Chairperson: Thank you Professor Kishore. We now invite Professor Chua to the stand.

Opposer: Actually, I have already lost the debate in this crowd even before I started, but anyway let me try to convince you otherwise. To begin with, how do we in fact come to have this topic of debate? And the reason I would suggest is that apparently we have consensus among Singaporeans in the past, and this consensus has been the basis of our economic development and of our present success, which probably explains the sentiments in the first voting round. And some would like to return to that state and perpetuate it in view of the gathering pace of public contentions and challenges to official policies on many fronts, probably for 20 years now, although most people think that it is a 2011 phenomenon. The different fronts that public policies have been challenged have been on income inequality, gender inequality, nature of capital punishment, intensified religiosity and the total population. I would suggest that that was not as particular as Kishore said, an abnormal moment in the history of Singapore.

So what we have therefore is a past of consensus but an emerging presence of contentions. The question is: Did we really have consensus without contention even during the rapid economic growth phases, even during the 40 years of context that Kishore refers to? Firstly, contestations were suppressed very forcefully from the early 1960s to about the mid-1970s, a period which most of us would like to forget about because it is a period marked by excesses of authoritarian repressions. Dissent was therefore suppressed, lay dormant, but did not disappear. Secondly, economic development programmes have provided full employment, public housing, mass education, improved public health, and overall improvements of the rising standards of living. For a population that had been living with chronic unemployment and material deprivation, what was there not to like? What was there not to agree with the economic development program? What was there to contest?

If there was a consensus, it was because citizens had by that time weighed up the benefits to their lives. They had quietly debated among themselves, and within themselves, the options, and agreed that the government policies of that time were better than... to improve their lives, and therefore supported it. But, had contention therefore disappeared, as some people might suggest? The governed will always want to be heard, and always want to hear different proposals so that they can come to an informed decision. Contention may then remain invisible until a specific public policy is obviously unacceptable.

So, for an example, in the midst of the supposed consensus, at the peak of the popularity of Mr Lee Kuan Yew, the government foisted on the population, the graduate mothers policy. The people protested, and protested very, very loudly. The ones who protested the most and the loudest were in fact the graduate women who stood to benefit from the policy but were indignant about the blatant class discrimination against their lesser-educated counterparts. There is an ethical and moral system at work, not just the economy. This very significant protest against the graduate mothers policy should have put paid to any assumption that Singaporeans are not thinking people, and simply following the dictate of the ruling government, a simplistic impression that misrecognised the citizens' agreement with the government policies as political docility. This misrecognition was at one time so widespread that it even caused Kishore himself to ask rhetorically, "Can Asians think?" — including Singaporeans, of course.

So we should remind ourselves that no genuine consensus can be obtained without prior contention. Without prior debate of differences, any so-called agreement is merely simply an imposition on those over whom we have power: Men over women, bosses over employees, government over the governed. Such impositions will always leave dissatisfaction, unhappiness, and dissent and rebelliousness — suppressed but waiting for its moment to burst forth. If we desire consensus on public policies to secure Singapore's future, we will need to be more practised at contestation and contention in order to arrive at policies that we can all support.

If indeed we had an era of consensus, I would suggest that the age of contentions has already been with us for about two decades. The formulations of the shared values in 1991, from which the topic of debate undoubtedly derived, were the first attempt by the government to put a lid on the emerging contention age. But putting a lid on the pressure cooker might hold it for a while, but is ultimately futile. In the end, when the slew of government policies without consultation converged to produce a state of deterioration of many aspects of everyday life at the end of the last decade, the citizens spoke and spoke very loudly in 2001 GE — now widely known as the watershed that brought what is now called the "new normal".

And this new normal has already produced positive results. Government recognition of the problem of intensifying social and economic inequalities; a rethink of population density projection; the removal of mandatory capital punishment for drug trafficking; easing the pressure on children's education; and very significantly, the radical reduction of ministerial and presidential salaries — an imposition on the height of the PAP's power but an unhappiness among the citizens that took 20 years to finally be heard and acted upon. There has always been contention. Even the PAP and the Cabinet insist that there is no groupthink in the party and the government. Even if both project a united stand on every issue, after an agreement has been achieved, there is no avoiding even greater public debate and contention of issues on Singapore's future in the future.

Chairperson: Professor Chua, thank you. Your time is up. If you could just stay at the podium, let me ask you the first question, related to what you have just spoken about. You seemed to suggest that the last 10, 20 years have been about contest and contestation in Singapore. Are you suggesting then, that given Singapore's context in the changing world economy, that this is still the way to go, or, that it should be public contest, that debates and discussion should be made public and not so much behind the scenes?

Opposer: I am suggesting that the debate and the contestation have never gone away. It has always been there. It is the very nature of politics. It is the very nature of the relations between those who are governed and those doing the governing. The difference is in the past [is that] the forum of public airing of the differences was very limited to a single page of *The Straits Times*. And we all know what gets edited out of *The Straits Times*. So if there was a consensus, it was also partly manufactured by the absence of platforms. The Internet didn't just suddenly produce contentious Singaporeans. The Internet merely provides the unlimited space for all the differences that have been held at bay either forcefully or with the absence of forum. So I think that any assumption that we have been living in a consensus society is at best an illusion. The difference is that, now with the Internet, it is no longer able to keep the differences under wraps behind closed doors and project a common front.

Chairperson: Okay, thank you very much. Next question, Professor Kishore, would you like to take the mic at the podium. You talked about Singapore being an abnormal society. We are moving towards a more normal state of affairs. How is consensus, then, going to help Singapore develop as it becomes more normal as a society?

Proposer: Let me begin by surprising Beng Huat by agreeing with him. You know the last 40 years that you spoke about, 1971 to 2011, when you describe how in many ways, it was an era in which the government was making many of the key decisions, leading the debate, framing the issues, yes, it was very much a top-down era, I agree. But that is not what consensus is all about. And I am glad that just before I came up to the podium, I borrowed Choo Chiau Beng's iPad, and checked Wikipedia to make sure I understood the meaning of the word "consensus". The word "consensus" does not mean a top-down process but a bottom-up process. So I am not arguing, even though Beng Huat thinks I am, that we can go back to the days of 1971 to 2011 where you have a top-down process. That era is gone. You have a much more assertive, demanding population. Contestation is naturally rising. And it is in this context where contestation is naturally rising that you need consensus, because the context has changed. The needs have changed.

You can go back and argue about what was good or bad over the past 40 years, and arguments will carry on but those arguments are irrelevant because we will never ever go back to that era. So when you ask me, Debra, what is this new normal? This new normal means that we have a very different world globally and a very different world domestically. We have one of the best education systems in the world and therefore we have one of the best-educated populations in the world. Hence, they will no longer accept the kind of *diktat* that they, in the past, would have accepted. Now they expect to be consulted, they expect to be part of the decision-making process, and they want to be part of the consensus-making. That is why I keep emphasising that given today's different context, where you have pressures coming from outside and pressures coming from inside, if we just focus on contestation and accentuate the differences, then I fear that Singapore will be torn apart. I might tell you this is not a hypothetical fear. If I did a realistic scenario plan, and you know what scenario planning is about, I can easily describe to you a scenario where Singapore continues to go downhill. So in that context, in this different context, I assure you what we need today is more consensus.

Chairperson: Thank you Professor Kishore. I will now give Professor Chua a chance, eight minutes to take on Professor Kishore's arguments. He will do the questioning and after that it will be Kishore's turn to question Professor Chua. So Professor Chua, if you are ready.

Opposer: Yes. It is interesting. I actually agree with Kishore that the last 40 years have been abnormal. And as I said, the last 40 years have been abnormal because contestation had sort of disappeared, allowing us to believe that we live in a consensus society. It has disappeared to the point where Singaporeans were thought to be de-politicised, no longer political. In fact, as I said, when the opportunity for being political appeared, they took to it enthusiastically. But I think the abnormality is very interesting because that is why after 2011 when the term "new normal" was being bandied about, in the same Singapore Perspectives at that time, I had argued that we were simply ambling to what is the normal, rather than arriving at the new normal, because a society in which public debates were completely suppressed without any kind of opportunity for it to be aired is abnormal — in spite of its economic successes, in spite of its economic development, in spite of the massive improvement of material life of Singaporeans. So what are we heading towards? We are heading towards a more normal, democratic society. It is also, as Kishore would say, that contentions will become — not necessarily more intensified as he said it would be… but as I said, it has always been there but is now more public. And because it is more public, the decisions that finally have to be made will probably be supported much better, and also will not have to take 20 years for the unhappiness to be finally rectified, as in the case of the salaries of ministers.

Chairperson: Professor Chua, would you like to ask Professor Kishore a question directly?

Opposer: What I would like to know from Kishore, which is interesting is that he said that he is not asking for a return to a mythological past of consensus because, I think, as he knows, if we were to do that, it will be to engage in a nostalgia that is futile. Nostalgia, as you know, has no future. So we are talking about the future. We are talking about the future and we are talking about a future in which – as he says rightly – open expression of differences, open expression of different desires, different imaginings of what the world will become, will actually become intensified. And therefore, how do we arrive at a consensus other than through more debates and more public discussions, because to do otherwise would be to truncate that very process of open discussions, arriving in genuine consensus. But to do otherwise, would be to cut off the debate that is necessary, and to do so will, again as I said, leave behind a very unhappy citizenry in spite of growing wealth, not just growing wealth, but growing income equality.

So my question is: Is there any other way of arriving at a consensus that is desired without much more open debate, and without the fact that we should now, because of our 40 years of abnormal past, train ourselves to be able to deal with each other openly in our differences? We are all making references to Zainul, our good friend – I told Zainul that the problem, as a sociologist, of not being able to understand the Malay community in depth is that I was never given the real feeling about what the Malay community feels, because it has always been mediated by community leaders that are already handpicked, including two days ago when the Prime Minister said that he had an open, frank discussion behind closed doors. How frank and open can it be to the rest of us when we are not behind those closed doors? How are we expected to understand how the Malays feel if we are not part of that closed door? How are we going to, actually, come to an understanding that will in fact support, or not support the *tudung* issue? And if it is a national issue, it is not up to just the Malay community to resolve but all of us to resolve. But to do that, we have to learn to be able to handle differences publicly, and only then, as Kishore rightly says, consensus must be arrived at. In fact, all contentions, all contestations are to arrive at a consensus. The question is in the process, not the final outcome. I would like to know if there is any other formula of arriving at consensus without public debate and public contentions?

Chairperson: I think Kishore you have about one minute left to respond to that if you want.

Proposer: I have one minute?

Chairperson: It is the longest question I have heard, but yes.

Proposer: I have one minute to respond to a long question.

Opposer: Now you have 53 seconds.

Proposer: I would say that he used the very nice phrase, "the more normal democracy". That is a mythical world, a "more normal democracy". Is Thailand a more normal democracy?

Opposer: No.

Proposer: Right, I mean you have elections and the people reject the elections. Is Ukraine a democracy?

Opposer: You are picking all the wrong cases.

Proposer: Let me pick the United States of America.

Opposer: Is Western Europe a democracy?

Proposer: Is the United States of America a democracy? I was in Davos, and Tom Friedman, one of the world's most influential columnists says, how is it you can have a country like the United States of America, with two or three hundred years of political tradition, yet a small movement like the Tea Party hijacks the whole government and brings it to the edge of a precipice? Is that the more normal democracy? Is that what Beng Huat wants for Singapore?

Chairperson: Alright, Kishore, your time is up but guess what, you get a chance now to cross-examine Professor Chua, so you can ask him the question again and he has to respond this time. Because now you have eight minutes to cross-examine him.

Proposer: You know, as I listen to Beng Huat, to be fair, I am quite sympathetic to many of his criticisms of many mistakes that we have made. I think it is an absolute fact that Singapore is not a perfect society. We have made mistakes, and in fact the government also acknowledges it has made a lot of mistakes in the past few decades. But when you keep on banging your head against that past, you are wasting your time because that past is gone and cannot come back. As Beng Huat himself said, nostalgia is not about the future. And the future that is coming, I can guarantee you, is so different from what we had in the past four decades that to keep knocking your head against the past 40 years is an absolute waste of time. So my question to Beng Huat is, look at Singapore as it exists today and ask yourself a very simple question: What are the existing vulnerabilities in Singapore society that uninhibited contestation could worsen?

You know, when you have a society, and you have been using the word "CMIO" — 75% Chinese, 15% Malay, 6–8% Indian, and the rest, others — is it natural for such a society to naturally have harmony, or is it more natural to have divisions surface when you no longer have the kind of strong top-down environment providing a lid on the box and making sure that nothing gets out of hand? In the past, when someone made a racial insult or an ethnic slur, you could be sure that the government would come down like a tonne of bricks on him or her. Now that you no longer have a government that comes down like a tonne of bricks, what happens? Will these natural divisions surface again? This is why I believe that we have to pay attention to the fact that the era of normal democracies is gone. You mentioned wonderful Western Europe. How many of you saw an article, just two, three days ago in the *International New York Times*, of this wonderful happy society called Norway, which is one of the richest societies in the world, which has lots of money, lots of welfare, and guess what? A few hundred Muslims came into Norway and lived in the neighbourhood. And you know what happened? The Norwegians left that neighbourhood. This is an open, tolerant, happy, welfare society, very democratic, very advanced, but when you have these divisions, you can see what happens.

I can give you example after example in all corners of the world where things are falling apart. The United States is a strong example. I asked Martin Wolf, the chief financial correspondent of the *Financial Times*, when I was in Davos: "How would you characterise the mood in the West today?" He said it is a mood of deep pessimism. Most young people do not believe that the world of tomorrow will be better for them. In fact they live in a state of fear for the future and, as you know, extremist right-wing parties are emerging in Western Europe, in the land of advanced democracies. That is the new normal, these new divisions. If even the advanced democracies are being subjected to new stresses and strains, how can Chua Beng Huat so confidently predict that Singapore's democracy is so good that all these divisions will have no impact whatsoever on Singapore? What is your answer to that, Beng Huat?

Opposer: I am glad that the rising right wing of the world has been mentioned, and I think it is very serious and important issue. And I think that one of the mistakes that many Singaporeans make is to simply equate ourselves with those conditions. It is a very simple argument in Singapore that exists all the time — to say, if you give in on one of these, you are going to give in to a whole string of other things that come, so every decision is a slippery slope. I did some research work on drug rehabilitation, and the interesting thing is, well, some people use drugs but not everybody follows. We have to believe in the basic ability of ordinary citizens to reason. And as Kishore says, now expressions of difference are much more forcefully made on the Internet, and the government, wisely, is no longer there to police them, because we don't need the government to police them, because the other netizens on the Internet check them. And if you look at what is happening in the local media and media all over the world, the mainstream media is now tracking social media. It is not the other way around. If the debate goes on loud enough and long enough in the social media, the mainstream media would have to pick it up and the government would have to respond. The pressure is coming from the ground, not a group of people who presume the privilege position of knowledge, that just make the decision for our best interest. Our best interest is to be handled by ourselves.

As to the question of Islam, to the question of rising right wing, it is really rising right wing primarily directed at Muslims, and particularly a confusion between Muslims fundamentalism and ordinary Muslim individuals and families who just want to make a living. The reason I would suggest is because Europe has never seriously, in spite of its constant rhetoric of liberalism, seriously tried to understand Islam. Because within the rhetoric of liberalism is the constant belief that if we can talk long enough we would be able to resolve our differences. But there are some differences that are fundamental, that people's lives, people's definition of themselves depend on. If they should negotiate those fundamental beliefs, they wouldn't know what their lives' meanings are. I am proposing that in the case of Europe, Christian Europe had never really tried to understand that fundamental difference.

Chairperson: Thank you, Professor Chua. Your time is up. I would like to invite all of you to pick up your voting devices. We are going to take another dip stick here to see how convinced you were by the two debaters who agree with each other and take a second poll.

2ND VOTING RESULT:
PROPOSITION — 210, OPPOSITION — 331

Chairperson: Proposition: 210. Opposition 331. What a good shift. Maybe during this break we can all think about the questions you want to ask because the next session will be an open round where all of you will get a chance to throw your questions at either of the debaters. And the first poll that you see 274 were for the motion versus 210 now; and 187 for the opposition at that time versus 331 now. Quite a change.

Alright, anybody who would like to ask a question, please raise your hand and please come to the mic. And you can ask your questions to either of the speakers. Anyone with the first question?

Questioner 1: Thank you, Chair. In light of the watershed election that occurred just now, with the percentages going exactly the other way round, and in the spirit of open debate, I would like to ask each speaker to please, ask one question, the answer to which, would turn over his own arguments. So in other words, critique the other side, ask yourself one question that would overturn the conclusions you come to, in light of this watershed election.

Chairperson: Let them argue a case for the other side, right? That is what you are asking them to do.

Questioner 1: Yes, but they have to do it themselves.

Opposer: Why would I want to do that?

Questioner 1: Because it is the prerogative of the voters to ask the politicians to do exactly this. We are voters, we voted for them, so it is our prerogative, as a voter myself, I am asking them to critique themselves, so that we know which better truth emerges from this self-critique. One question.

Opposer: I still do not understand the logic of your question.

Questioner 1: It is very simple, Dean Mahbubani, please ask yourself a question that would overturn the conclusion that you come to, and the same for professor Chua.

Proposer: I must say I have great difficulty following your question. But anyway, I must say that I expected that the second round of voting to be reflected in the first round of voting. Beng Huat and I were discussing the voting at lunch. We were convinced that the majority of you would be in favour of contestation and not of consensus at the beginning. So he was surprised as I was that most of you were in favour of consensus at first and contestation later, which is in itself an interesting reflection of what is going on here. So the question I had in my mind is simply: Is the composition in this room reflective of the general population in Singapore? If you had, in a sense, a representative sample of the population of Singapore, what would they say? I actually think they would argue for more contestation. And the reason why they would argue for more contestation — again going back to my point about context — is that it is in reaction to what has happened over the last 40 years. And that is my concern. My concern is that, so much of the reaction in Singapore begins with what happened in the last 40 years, and we focus so much on the past, not realising that the future that is coming will be so different. So my general point is that the debate about contestation and consensus should look at what's coming in the future and not focus on what happened in the past.

Opposer: I agree, but except, as I said, I have a fundamental disagreement about the process. In the sense that, in the past, the reason why it is abnormal, there are several reasons why it is abnormal. One reason why it is abnormal is precisely the hidden nature of public debate. The absence of it, and creating, as I said, an illusion, and maybe even a complacency on the part of the government to believe that there is a consensus between them and the population. I agree that there was a consensus, but it was not a consensus of simply following, it was a consensus because the government policies were right. And if the government policies were right, and if we believe in the common rationality of individual rather than an elitism that presumes that rationality lies in the highly educated, there is every good reason to believe that reasonable citizens would have supported those policies even if there were public debates. That there was no need to artificially hide the debates behind closed doors. There is no need to conduct debate only among the educated and it could have been the publicly aired. And something like the ministerial salary wouldn't have passed. It wouldn't have carried on for 20 years of unhappiness among the people.

So what we are heading towards, as I said, I do not think that the debate, the contestation will intensify. I think that it has always been there. It has been intensified by speed of technology, not by production of dissent, not by production of difference. I think the differences were always there but always hidden. So now we better get practice in public debate, in open debate, because the mechanisms to hide it are gone and over. So heading towards the future, the future definitely has to be secured by more open contestations to arrive at a consensus that we can all support. Not we have a closed-door meeting, everybody went home happy. I never believed that every Malay leader went home happy after the closed-door sessions.

Chairperson: Alright, thank you very much.

Question 2: Professor Chua, I do not see how a debate about whether you can have a play on a woman, a Malay Muslim woman or an Indian Muslim woman, say, she would like to divorce her husband that, it would be a public play, and that there would be another group that says, go right ahead and do it publicly, and then, if we have a controversy about it, that this can be done publicly and everyone will go away happy. I mean, somehow, because they had a contest about that. I do not think that one group that feels disrespected will walk away and say, you know, nothing has been done about it. I don't see how a debate about the weighting of mother tongue, or specifically, Mandarin, and whether we can change, can be had publicly and then some consensus would emerge. I mean I can only see contestation, and if you say that we need to practise publicly and find a way to establish the middle ground, I do not see how that is going to happen. Except if we start off and we say we value consensus and we must agree to disagree, and that we establish principles for consensus finding, that we would be able to have those public debates and even allow, you know, have the disrespected group walk away happily. So I find it difficult just to rest that, your case, and I find that the end point is really the other side of it. Could you please respond?

Opposer: Yes let me... because there are two examples and I do not want to take up too much time. Let me use the second case on the question of Mandarin. Anyone in this room who has ever been to a public seminar conducted in Mandarin would undoubtedly come away feeling the unhappiness of the Chinese community that is committed to Chinese culture. It is now a language that is no longer viable in public. It is now in a situation where the so-called bilingualism produces young people who cannot make a single sentence in one single language — half in Mandarin, and half in English, because they are competent in neither languages. It is a situation where there is always someone in the audience who would confront the speakers on stage about how the government had let Chinese language, Chinese culture, atrophy to a point where it is now no longer viable. There are more students from Malaysia studying in Taiwan than Singaporeans. There are few Singaporeans now who really are able to go to a Chinese-medium university. All these have been the result of an insistence that English should be the common language among Singaporeans. All these have been [due to] the policy based, on a very mistaken idea, that polyglot ability is not good. So all the dialects must disappear in order to teach Mandarin and a Mandarin that is progressively watered down to the point where you can take second language as Mandarin B. In Hokkien they say *jiat-liao-bi* (meaning "useless"). It is a total waste of time because it has been pressured by parents who find their children having trouble learning Mandarin, to the point that, it used to be an important qualification to go to university — it now does not count. So if you said because we did not have public debate, is this the result because we didn't have public debate about language policy? Did we produce happier people? If we had an open debate about language policy, would Chinese have deteriorated to the current standard? We do not know. So the thing is, in the current situation, would Singapore have been a happier place if there were public debate? It is counter factual and can no longer be proven. We will have to see how the future unfolds if we embark on a more open discussion society.

Chairperson: Professor Kishore, do you want to respond in any way to that?

Proposer: Well, actually I am glad that Beng Huat has brought up this very difficult subject of language policy, because that is an example of what could have been very different in Singapore. It was a very brave decision by the government to say that the common language should be English. Now believe me, if we had gone the way of Sri Lanka where the government decided that the common language should be Sinhalese and deprived the Tamils of even using their own language — leading to 30 years of civil war in Sri Lanka. That is what the choice of language is all about.

And if you imagine a Singapore in which, as a result of mass voting, you asked people to vote, [the] majority to vote, "What would you want your first language of Singapore to be?" And if the majority democratically selects and says, "Hey, we want Mandarin to be the first language of Singapore, to be the official functioning language of Singapore." That is also possible. Democratically through a process of discussion, we will end up with that result. What kind of Singapore would that be? Would it be the Singapore we have today? Or would it be a very divided Singapore? This is my point about the fact that for 40 years, we have been living in a very special bubble where we did not have to confront all these hard issues which, frankly, every other society has been confronting.

And if you look again at what the "normal" is, whenever the issue of language surfaces politically, it almost never leads to a consensus. It almost always leads to divisions. And that is why Beng Huat is right. In theory, we are much better off. Let us have an open discussion. Let us have democratic selection, but trust me, you may not like the results. The results may be, in Singapore, the exact opposite of what we have seen today, and all you have to do, by the way, is a very simple test. If you are a political scientist, you want to use all the knowledge of social science to help you make a decision. Look around the world at all the multiethnic societies, and look at what decisions they make on language and how they made them, and then you can see the result. Yes, it is a fact that English was imposed on Singapore's society, but the fact that it was imposed led to a situation where you have Malays, Chinese, and Indians in this room who feel a sense of community because there is a common language that exists. But if the opposite had happened and you had a very populist politician like Thaksin Shinawatra emerge in Singapore, and he says, "I can feel the pain of the majority community, who feel that they have been cut off from their culture and their roots because they have not been allowed to use their language fully," what would the result be? And should that kind of politician emerge in the next 10 years, I wouldn't be surprised at all, because that is the nature of politics. Look at a society like Yugoslavia. Why did Yugoslavia suddenly go from being one of the most peaceful, multiethnic societies, to splintering into four or five different nation states? Because they suddenly had democracy, and Slobodan Milosevic said, "Hey, we are the dominant community, we are the Serbs, we must exert ourselves, we the Serbs should be in charge." And all the Serbs voted for him and the country fell apart.

So all I ask you to do is to look around at any other multiethnic society. Forget about the dominant societies with a single language, they have it very easy. Just look around the world and use as your laboratory specimens the live, existing multiethnic societies — and tell me a happy story that comes from people choosing a language that represents the majority and ignores the minority. We are very fortunate that we did not make that decision but if you allow people like Chua Beng Huat to bring out the language monster up again, I would say be careful!

Chairperson: Thank you Professor Kishore. I am going to give the floor one last question to ask to either of them. The gentlemen over there at the corner.

Question 3: I am a student from Raffles Institution. To Dr Kishore Mahbubani, to what extent do we value consensus in order to make a decision? Should we wait for all sectors of the society to come to a consensus? Should society and government agree fully? For instance, in the casino issue, society largely agreed that we should not build them. However, the government went ahead despite the consensus. So, to what extent do we regard the consensus as important in the decision-making process? And to Dr Chua, as what Dr Kishore has mentioned, contestation does not necessarily lead to consensus. For example, on the 377A issue, society has remained divided and the government has effectively put off the problem, saying that we need greater consensus, but there is no resolution in sight. So to what extent should we regard contestation as the means towards how we should be able to make a decision?

Chairperson: So he asked how important is consensus in decision-making, you are citing the casino issue as an example where the government went ahead even though society didn't think it should have. That is your view of it. That was for Professor Kishore. And for Professor Chua, how do you create a resolution when there is no resolution in sight for an issue like 377A, [where] the government seems to have diffused the situation and there is still no solution.

Proposer: I want to begin by saying that achieving consensus is not an easy thing. I emphasised that it is a bottom-up process and not a top-down process. And I actually think that, you know, two words in Indonesian describe the situation very well: *musyawarah* and *mufakat*, "deliberation" and "consensus". Everybody is consulted, you talk to people, and you arrive at a decision. By definition, a consensus is something that does not please everybody, because everybody has to give up something. If you all stick to your own position, there will be no consensus. A consensus actually comes about when everybody compromises. That is what it is about. The casino example is an interesting one. You may be right, if there is a referendum in Singapore, and if the population comes out very strongly against the casino, it is possible that the license may not be renewed when it is over. By the way, I was personally very opposed to the casino decision because I actually had a father who was a compulsive gambler and got into deep trouble because of gambling. Hence, this is an example where if you had a consensual decision-making process, Singaporeans could say, no more casinos.

Opposer: Let me first talk about Yugoslavia. Yugoslavia fell apart. Yes it fell apart because Yugoslavia was always held together artificially by an imposition of a communist party. And the communist party in government destroyed all civil society linkages among the population. So when the party collapses, the different groups in Yugoslavia had no other means of reorganising themselves, except to fall back to the most primordial basis of reorganising. And at that point, there was no structure at all for possible negotiations. In which case, the result was the kind of civil war that we saw.

I am saying that in normal society, in a society in which, if there were no coercive imposition, and if the society were allowed to develop ties, civic ties beyond race, beyond religion. Yugoslavia would not have fallen apart so quickly if it were to fall apart at all. So we do see very serious differences in democratic societies where differences have taken root and differences have become entrenched, but they do not fall apart. They muddled along. That is what they are supposed to do. The Tea Party held the government for a while. But they did not win America. They are now in somewhat of a retreat, none of their candidates now are electable as presidential candidates for the Republican Party in the next election to come. So we have to have faith over a longer stretch of time and not be in a hurry to always impose a decision. We have to have faith to have the debate sounded out. At some point, everyone, given their self-interest, will in fact give and take some, and not be completely entrenched. On the case of 377A, it is not going away. The kind of adjustment that have been made — to say that we will keep it in the law book for a symbolic stand on value, but we will not actively pursue its application — is simply a short-term solution. It is simply a short-term solution that satisfies nobody, and furthermore, to have a law in the book that will not be activated makes a mockery of the law. Why would you want a law that you are never going to use? And if it is there, there is always a chance that it may be used when convenient, or when necessary. So we would better off to come to a decision and take it out. And because it will be challenge constantly, over and over again, and it is going to cause the public a lot of money to continuously defend a law that we no longer want to use, it seems so absurd, does it not? So, is there no solution to 377A? Yes, there is. It is just that we are not taking it.

Chairperson: Thank you, Professor Chua. We are now going to give each of the speakers three minutes for their closing arguments, as we are running out of time and the first person to go will be the opposer, which is Professor Chua. Your time starts now.

Opposer: No society, no modes of government can run without debate between the people, between those who are governed and those who are doing the governing. That is what we mean by consensus. Neither Kishore nor I disagree on that point. We believe that society has to run on consensus. Where we disagree is how this consensus is arrived at. Whether this consensus should be arrived at by public debate with as much time as necessary, or whether the debate should be truncated in some way or another, either through our impatience for which we are famously known, to want to have instant results in every aspect of our lives. Either through our impatience or through our fear, precisely, to our imagined fear that people will take extreme positions — and so therefore, we keep them behind closed doors. That kind of preemptive action is not very viable because the logical thing to say is, "If it did not have a chance to take place, how do you know it will not work?" So we are always making very preemptory kinds of decisions based on the fear that things will go bad. You have to have more faith.

In 50 years, we have not gone berserk. And every time the race riot is mentioned… I would like to remind you that we have not had a race riot since 1964. That is a long time. We have not had a riot for so long that we do not know how to cope with the Little India melee. We still insist on calling it a riot. We have gotten to a point where we really cannot cope with events. So I think my suggestion is that: in the last 40 years, we have lost our ability to be practised in public discussions — in public discussion with the right attitude and in public discussion with the idea that eventually we will have to live with ourselves, together, and not as entrenched differences. Currently, the differences are not public; they are hidden. We do not even know what the differences are. And therefore, a member of the audience said, "Do

Singaporeans understand Malays really?" No, we do not. Because we have never had proper access to how they feel, how they think. How is Islam, in some ways, different from all the rest of us who are striving like crazy, and living a life of constant stress? So, that is my point. My point is, not because we don't need consensus, but we need the process of arriving at consensus to be changed for the future.

Chairperson: Thank you, Professor Chua. Professor Kishore, your time starts now.

Proposer: Well, Beng Huat was right. We agree that the people should decide. That is not what the discussion is about. It is about how we decide. He would like a process of public contestation. I say let us have consultation and discussion. And his position on 377A completely contradicts his earlier argument. His argument is: Let us have contestation on 377A, let the people vote.

If you had a vote on 377A, you know what is going to happen? People will say, stick with the law and implement it. It will be a much harder line and tougher position, and our gay community will suffer because of this contestation and voting. And he wants to walk away from that kind of difficult situation on the mythical assumption that if you had contestation and voting, we will naturally end up in harmony. Let me just give you two or three examples. Look at the current mood against foreigners in Singapore. You saw what happened to Anton Casey? One Facebook post and, boom, he is out of Singapore. You like that kind of thing? How many foreigners are you going to expel from Singapore? Let us have more contestation. Where will Singapore be without these foreigners?

Look at the mood about rising inequality in Singapore. It is a concern all over the world. Populism is rising. It is rising all over the world. It is rising in America, and it is rising in Europe. And if you have contestation, they will say, let us tax all these rich people, take away their bungalows, and kick them out of Singapore. And where will Singapore be? So, in this kind of environment where you are getting a more difficult, more fractious environment emerging in Singapore, you unleash Chua Beng Huat, and you get him to push for more contestation. I tell you, you will not be happy with the results. Thank you very much.

Chairperson: Alright, your time is up. Thank you very much to both gentlemen. You can take a seat. Can I once again encourage all of you to pick up your voting devices and we will take a final poll to see who swayed whom the most?

3RD VOTING RESULT:
PROPOSITION — 316, OPPOSITION — 232

The proposition has won back the poll, swinging it back from 210 to 316. The opposition is now at 232, and the electorate has increased to, once again, without any boundaries, to 548 from 541 earlier. Congratulations to both of them. A big round of applause, please, to the team. A very, very interesting debate. I am sure you will all agree this has been the most interesting discussion that we have ever had at a conference. We have both debaters agreeing with each other most of the time, except in the last five minutes when they had to put on a bit of drama. So thank you all very much for your attention.

13

Sovereignty for Small States

BILAHARI KAUSIKAN

What does "sovereignty" mean to a small country such as Singapore? We did not seek independence but had independence thrust upon us. I have been told that Mr Lee Kuan Yew once said, "Small island states are a political joke." That quote implies a concept of sovereignty based on which our founding fathers sought independence within Malaysia rather than alone.

I suspect it was difficult for that generation to even conceive of Singapore as anything but a part of what was then called Malaya. Obviously, and thankfully, that concept of sovereignty was proved mistaken or was rendered mistaken by the Herculean efforts of our pioneer generation. And by that, I do not mean just our leaders, but our entire people.

The concept of sovereignty is constantly evolving. Rather than try to define the elephant, I propose to take its existence for granted and instead consider what sovereignty means to Singapore by analysing a single sentence, and that sentence is this: "Singapore is a small state located in South-east Asia."

This seems straightforward, but is it really? What do we mean by "small"? We are, of course, a physically small country and a moderately athletic person could walk across it in a day without too much difficulty. But as a trading centre, as a logistics hub, as a port and airport and as a financial centre, among other things, we are far from "small". In trade, connectivity and finance, among others, we loom quite large internationally, far larger than our physical size may lead one to expect.

Sir Stamford Raffles established modern Singapore as a trading centre in 1819. And I read somewhere that by 1898, or thereabouts, our trade was larger than that of Japan, larger than that of what was then called the Dutch East Indies, and was exceeded only by China. Some recent archaeological studies suggest that we may have been a significant trading centre since the 14th century, even before the concept of sovereignty in its current form existed.

Trade requires connectivity; it requires logistics and finance. Of course, today, we perform these functions at a far higher level of sophistication and complexity than in the past. But the point is that they are essentially similar functions and we have performed them as a British colony, as part of Malaysia and only in the past 50 years — which is but the blink of an eyelid in the sweep of history — as a sovereign and independent country.

There is, therefore, no reason to assume that sovereignty and independence are necessary conditions to enable us to perform such functions. We could conceivably do so even if our independence and sovereignty were, by some blunder of policy, accident of politics or malicious whim of the gods, severely compromised.

Size — physical size — does matter. And small states are intrinsically irrelevant to the workings of the international system. It is impossible to imagine a world without large countries such as the United States, China, India, Indonesia, Brazil or Russia, or even without medium-sized states such as Australia, Japan, France or Germany. But the world would probably get along fine without Singapore as a sovereign and independent country. After all, it has only had to put up with us for 50 years. For small states, relevance is not something that can be taken for granted, but rather an artefact — created by human endeavour, and once created, preserved by human endeavour. The creation and maintenance of relevance must be the overarching strategic objective of small states.

The majority of states are small. Slightly more than two decades ago, Singapore established the Forum of Small States (FOSS) at the United Nations; "small" being somewhat arbitrarily defined as having a population of 10 million or less. It now has 105 members out of a total UN membership of 193 states. The international relevance of many FOSS members is defined primarily by their vote within the UN. A vote in the UN is only that. It is not to be sneezed at but it is still only one vote. Singapore is exceptional as a small country in that our international identity and relevance is something more than just our UN vote. We have options beyond our single UN vote, and that is why we were able to establish FOSS in the first place.

How do we create relevance? There is no magic formula. What makes us relevant vis-à-vis country A may be irrelevant vis-à-vis country B and may become irrelevant to both A and B as well as C in a week or a month or a year or a decade. What is relevant will eventually become irrelevant and must therefore be continually refreshed.

The world is constantly changing and since the world will not change to suit our conveniences, we will have to constantly adapt to it. Since the future is unknowable, adaptation requires nimbleness of thought and action. Such thought and action need to be based on a clinical — some say cold-blooded — understanding of the world as it is and not as we think it ought to be. Even if we hope to change the world, we must first understand it without illusions because hope, however fervent, is never enough.

The bedrock of relevance is success. I have always told our Foreign Service Officers (FSOs) that if Singapore's foreign policy has been successful to some degree, it is not because of their good looks, it is not due to their natural charm, it is not due to the genius of their intellect. The most brilliant idea of a small country can be safely disregarded, if inconvenient, whereas the stupidest idea of a large country must be taken seriously. In fact, the stupider the idea the more seriously it must be taken because of the harm a large country can do. So if our FSOs succeed, it is only because Singapore as a country is successful. Singapore's success invests our ideas and actions with credibility.

Success must be defined, first of all, in economic terms. Will a barren rock ever be taken seriously? I know that it has become fashionable in certain circles to claim that economic success is not everything and that there are other worthy goals in life. I do not disagree as far as individuals are concerned. If any of our compatriots chooses to drop out of the rat race and devote his or her life to art or music or religion or even just to *lepak*, or relax, in one corner, I respect their choice and wish them well.

However, the country as a whole does not have this luxury. A world of sovereign states is, in fact, a rat race, and often a vicious one, in which the weak go to the wall. There can be no opting out for a sovereign state. To be crass, small countries will always have fewer options than large countries but rich small countries have more options than poor small countries and that tilts the scales in our favour. This is crucial because a small country cannot be only ordinarily successful. If we were no different from our neighbourhood, why should anyone want to deal with us rather than our larger neighbours who, moreover, are well endowed with natural resources? To be relevant, we have to be extraordinary. Being extraordinary is a strategic imperative.

And that brings me to the second part of the sentence with which I began. Singapore is not just a small country, but a small country in South-east Asia — not the South Pacific or South America or Europe or, thankfully, the Middle East. This seems obvious but I think this fact is nevertheless insufficiently appreciated, even by those who ought to know better.

A year or so ago, I was flabbergasted and disturbed when asked — asked in all seriousness and not just to take the mickey out of me (if it had been just to take the mickey out of me, it would have been acceptable) — by a Singaporean PhD candidate in political science why Singapore could not pursue a foreign policy akin to that of Denmark or Switzerland. The question aroused all my prejudices about the academic study of international relations. It makes a vast, and I thought glaringly obvious difference where a country is located. That a Singaporean PhD candidate, who presumably knew something about her own country as well as the subject she was studying, could ask such a question made me worry about the future of our country.

South-east Asia is not a natural region, by which I mean a region that can be defined by something intrinsic to itself. For example, Europe can be defined as heir to Christendom and the Roman Empire. The main characteristic of South-east Asia is diversity, which is another way of saying that there is nothing intrinsic to itself.

There are obvious differences of political form and levels of economic development. However, the most important diversities of South-east Asia are visceral: they are diversities of race, language and religion. These are the roots of political tension within and between the countries of South-east Asia. The Association of South-east Asian Nations (ASEAN) was set up with the intention, among other things, to mitigate these diversities to ensure a modicum of order and civility in interstate relationships in a region where this was not to be taken for granted. ASEAN has been reasonably successful. However, ASEAN can never entirely erase these primordial diversities because race, language and religion are the essence of core identities.

Singapore defines itself as a multiracial meritocracy and we organise ourselves on the basis of these principles. We are not perfect — there is no perfection to be found this side of heaven — but we take these principles seriously. They are what make Singapore, Singapore. They also make us extraordinary because our neighbours organise themselves on the basis of very different principles.

This is most obvious in the case of Malaysia. It was the irreconcilable contradiction between fundamentally different political philosophies — multiracial meritocracy in our case and Malay dominance politely enshrined in Article 153 of the Malaysian Constitution as "the special position of the Malays" — that made it impossible for us to remain in Malaysia. No matter how closely we cooperate — and despite occasional spats, we do cooperate very closely in many areas — it would be impossible for us to be part of Malaysia ever again unless Malaysia were to abandon its basic organising principle. And if you believe that will happen, there is a bridge I can let you have really cheap.

The essential issue is existential; not what we do, but what we are — a Chinese-majority country with neighbours whose own Chinese populations are typically less than fully welcome minorities and whose attitudes towards their own Chinese populations are too often projected upon us. The very existence of a Chinese-majority multiracial meritocracy that has been extraordinarily successful compared with its neighbours is often taken as an implicit criticism of differently-organised systems. That we are a tiny speck on the map and have hardly any history to speak of is an additional affront.

The intensity of such attitudes waxes and wanes; it manifests itself in different ways, at different times. But it never disappears because it is the structural consequence of the dynamic between different types of systems. Being extraordinary does not make us loved, but it is the price we must pay for survival and autonomy.

In different forms and various degrees, such attitudes exist throughout South-east Asia and in China, Japan and even Western countries such as Australia and the US. Examples spring to mind all too readily but diplomatic prudence does not permit me to elaborate, at least not too much.

Of course, none of this is intended to imply that we cannot work with our neighbours or any other country. Obviously we must, obviously we can and obviously we do and indeed, I dare say, we do so quite well. But these complexities are never going to go away and we ignore or deny them only at the peril of compromising our autonomy, that is to say, our sovereignty.

I believe that matters are going to get even more complicated because the external environment and our domestic environment are both changing and external and internal complexities will act and react with each other in ways that cannot be predicted.

There are already signs of foreign policy being used for partisan political purposes. This is probably inevitable. Domestic debates over foreign policy are not necessarily a bad thing provided that they take place within parameters defined by shared assumptions. Otherwise, it is playing with fire. At the very least, it degrades the nimbleness of our responses if we have to argue everything out anew from first principles.

Shared assumptions come naturally, almost unconsciously, to countries with long histories. But with only 50 years of shared history, I am not entirely confident that this is the case in Singapore. There is something of an intellectual vacuum that is being largely filled by nonsense.

We need to be better at educating ourselves about our own history. In my opinion, we are not doing a good enough job and the recent debates about our own political history are, unfortunately, notable only for their utter vacuity. What passes for critical thinking about our history is too often simply crying white if the establishment says black. Furthermore, social media exacerbates the situation by conflating information with opinion and treating both as entertainment.

As our domestic political environment becomes more complex with not only traditional political parties but also civil society organisations and advocacy groups espousing various causes contending in the policy space, opportunities for external influence will multiply.

Since the beginning of recorded history, states have always tried to influence each other, legitimately and openly through diplomacy but also oftentimes by covert means. The lines are not always clear and are likely to become even more blurred. The enthusiasm of some, mainly Western, diplomats to whip the heathen — that's us by the way — along the path of righteousness have already occasionally led them to cross the boundaries of legitimate diplomatic activity.

More fundamentally, market forces are creating economic spaces that transcend national boundaries, most notably between China and South-east Asia. This is to be welcomed on economic grounds but will have political and strategic consequences. It is redefining Westphalian notions of "state" and interstate relations and is putting stress on ASEAN as powerful centrifugal forces pull members in different directions.

As the only Chinese-majority country in South-east Asia, it could pose special challenges for Singapore. Already, Chinese diplomats and officials too often refer to Singapore as a "Chinese country". We politely, but firmly, tell them that they are mistaken. And we will continue to do so. But the implications are worth pondering.

14

Pragmatism Should Be Retained As Singapore's Governing Philosophy

KISHORE MAHBUBANI, TONG YEE, VIKRAM KHANNA AND EUGENE K B TAN

The motion for the Singapore Perspectives 2015 debate was "This conference resolves that pragmatism remains important and should be retained as our governing philosophy". During the course of the debate, members of the audience were invited to use their polling devices to vote for either the Proposition or the Opposition. The debate was chaired by Ms Debra Soon, Head of News Segment at MediaCorp.

Chairperson: Good afternoon, ladies and gentlemen. Welcome to the first "post-lunch slump" session of Singapore Perspectives 2015. I will do my best to keep the session moving along so you don't fall asleep but it will mainly be up to the erudite speakers to scintillate you as they debate a rather complex and convoluted motion. I have to say though, only a mind similarly complex and convoluted as Mr Janadas Devan's could have come up with this. The motion reads: "This conference resolves that pragmatism remains important and should be retained as our governing philosophy". Now since Mr Devan has arm-twisted me into this, I thought I could crack a joke at his expense. Actually maybe two, so if I'm not here next year, you all will know the reason why.

Now, to me, the motion assumes several things. First, that pragmatism is currently in place, is a governing philosophy and is ours, in other words, shared. Is pragmatism really a philosophy? Is this what has driven us as a collective and as a people? Or does this refer to the government, or the ruling party or both? Is it whatever works? Do policy efficiencies and outcomes justify pragmatic means? Has it always been our governing philosophy or has this evolved over the years? These are some thoughts to ponder. I'm sure our speakers will enlighten us. Here is a little on the format. We will have opening remarks, five minutes for each team, followed by a challenge and rebuttal round. The questions will be one-minute long and responses two minutes each. We will have four rounds.

It is my pleasure to introduce the teams to you. For the Proposition, we have Mr Tong Yee, Director of The Thought Collective, and Professor Kishore Mahbubani, Dean of Lee Kuan Yew School of Public Policy. For the Opposition, we have Mr Vikram Khanna, Associate Editor of *Business Times*, and Associate Professor Eugene Tan, School of Law, Singapore Management University. You have seen all of them on television and they are experts. The first thing that I have to do is to ask all of you to vote on the poll question — which is a bit sharper than the motion — "Pragmatism should be retained as Singapore's governing philosophy". Those of you who agree, in other words with the Proposition, vote "1" and send it in. Those of you who disagree, press "2" and send it in.

1ST VOTING RESULT:
PROPOSITION — 72.9%, OPPOSITION — 27.1%

Chairperson: Nearly 73 per cent feel that pragmatism has to be retained as our governing philosophy. Without further ado, I will now invite the first speaker of the Proposition, Tong Yee, to make his opening remarks. Tong Yee, your time starts now.

Tong Yee: Good afternoon. Honestly, the sheer fact that I'm standing here at the IPS Singapore Perspectives Conference debating with the brightest minds in Singapore is perhaps one of the least pragmatic things I've agreed to do in the past few years. Being a two-time repeat student, and having only earned a pass degree at NUS, this being in Theatre Studies mind you, I really do not know what insane and logical point I'm trying to prove by potentially making a fool of myself on national TV. So in preparation for this, I had time to seriously reflect and consider and I came to the conclusion that if I'm going to make the best of this learning opportunity, if I'm going to use this platform to make some profoundly poignant points that will somehow make Singapore proud, then I might as well win while I'm doing it, which is why I'm on Kishore's side and not the other side.

But that really is a point in itself. I've been a social entrepreneur for over a decade now, and when IPS first invited me to be a debater in this conference, I was politely given a choice of which side I would prefer to argue on. I chose to argue for pragmatism. Five to six years ago, I would even have surprised myself. One would think that social entrepreneurs are bold, innovative radicals, full of ideals and having a genuine desire to serve the community and do so in a very sustainable way. It is a bold and compelling dream and immensely fashionable among young people today. But at least in part, these ideals have held true for me, but maybe not so much in recent years.

The path of social entrepreneurship, if anything, has been a real education on the profound value of pragmatism. For me at least, there is a grounding principle on which I choose to live. I learnt very quickly in my very own pursuit of ideals that I really shouldn't keep falling from my own heights. Saving the world, wanting equality for all, making Singapore a place where people could all have equal opportunity, these were some things that I felt I needed to contribute to, partly due to my own suffering as I grew up as a young person in Singapore. But being able to deliver on that particular promise, on that particular social promise, to retain the integrity of being able to serve others is something that I quickly learnt was dependent upon sound financial principles, a strong grasp of reality, the accurate reading of current market conditions and, yes, taking into account the myriad personalities and working partners and collaborators that we have to somehow begin to work with. And if I genuinely wanted to pursue a career, to live my ideals, then I must first ground that in the practical reality. It's not the most popular thing to say, but one I believe we all have to hear and maybe have the courage to follow.

Make no mistake, we need idealism, we need inspiration and we need values. But pragmatism and us believing and wanting to achieve a world that is better than the one we currently have are not mutually exclusive. Rather it is pragmatism that remains a foundation for idealism. In the same way that it was our parents and pioneer generation that focused on pragmatic jobs that gave us, perhaps, the ability to follow our ideals today. It is very much similar to a generation of shipyard workers that followed, that allowed for today's cupcake makers. I do not find pragmatism to be an option that invites cynicism. In fact, pragmatism demands exceptional leadership and moral courage.

Pragmatism is not an expedient reading of any one given context and simply adapting ourselves to suit the demands of the times. Pragmatism is the reading of all contexts. It includes the moral one, financial one, political one, the cultural one and, yes, the sustainable one. And I have come to a conclusion that it's really the way of seeing things which perhaps would guarantee us the best success in the long game. Can the government stand against inequalities when the very nature of the world is unequal? I know that these are key narratives for campaigns and even elections. But for governance, I'm not so sure. I've found that when governments start wearing the underpants on the outside of the red and blue leotard and start flying around fighting for causes, they tend to look very ridiculous, at least eventually. No matter how hard I want to believe that we have shaken off the fact that we remain one of the smallest nation states in the world.

Has our success in supplying water for ourselves deceived us into thinking that we have somehow resolved the food problem or our complete dependence on others for food? Have our stellar education and the fact that we can hold debates in fancy hotels convinced us that our thoughts and perspectives are some things that will even be heard in a politically mired landscape? When push comes to shove, can Singapore really afford to push back and somehow still keep these wings on which we fly? Pragmatism is hardly popular, rarely inspiring and oftentimes sobering. But what it guarantees is that pragmatic leaders are grounded in realities and not ideologies. Thank you.

Chairperson: Thank you, Tong Yee. Can I now invite the first speaker for the Opposition, Vikram, to speak?

Vikram Khanna: Good afternoon, ladies and gentlemen, I have to say that were it not for Janadas' persuasive powers, I would not be here. I am participating in this debate with some trepidation. I mean, to argue against pragmatism in the context of Singapore is like arguing against motherhood, as you can see from the voting results. I have just five minutes so I can only sketch some broad themes, which I hope we can flesh out a little later. One doesn't oppose pragmatism. It is good. I think the first part of the motion is taken. Pragmatism is useful by definition. But the motion says it should be retained as our governing philosophy, not that it should be an important element in our governing philosophy, nor that our governing philosophy should be tempered with pragmatism but pragmatism should be it. That is it and nothing else. Now that kind of sticks in my throat a little bit.

I don't know if you saw the interview that the Prime Minister gave to the media a few days ago when he was asked about pragmatism and he said pragmatism is good, whatever works is good. But there are certain things that are what he calls "unshakeable". The rule of law, meritocracy, interethnic harmony, these are there forever, not out of pragmatism but because they are good intrinsically in and of themselves. And I think that there are certain things in life that are good intrinsically in and of themselves.

The other word in the motion that I have a problem with is that we should retain pragmatism. As if we have always been pragmatic. I know a lot of things have been sold as pragmatism, packaged as pragmatism, framed as being pragmatic. But I think we need to raise a few questions as to whether they really have been. I can say this in the context of, just to give a few examples which I hope we can flesh out later, our approach to welfare, housing, immigration and education, and our approach to information. These are some of the areas where I think we have sometimes been short of being pragmatic.

The other issue I have with the motion is pragmatism for whom? What is pragmatic for me might not be pragmatic for you. You can say pragmatic for society yes, but I think as society becomes more diverse and more complex, it becomes a much more difficult proposition to deliver on. There are also issues relating to our economic policy of the past; I think we have taken some very bold, visionary, radical steps. Our pro-multinational industrialisation programme of the 1960s went against the ruling paradigm of the time. We took big, bold bets in areas such as semiconductors and biotech. Some of these were quite radical decisions. In retrospect, they may appear to be pragmatic, but at the time when the decisions were made, they certainly were not. Some of them were leaps in the dark.

When we talk about the economy, we also need to look at the future, we need to look at innovation, we need to look at creativity, and these require things beyond just pragmatism. I hope we will be able to make a case for that.

But at the end of the day, I think I hope we can make the case that yes, pragmatism is important, but it also needs to be accompanied by other things, by idealism, inspiration, principle, conviction and a moral compass. Pragmatism alone is not enough.

I think I would recast the motion to say we need a pragmatic approach to our governing philosophy. That is completely different from saying pragmatism should be our governing philosophy. What it means is yes, we have elements of pragmatism but we also have elements of principle, we also have elements of morality and elements of conviction, and we also have elements of compassion and justice. If we say pragmatism alone should be our governing philosophy, I think we are elevating pragmatism itself to the level of an ideology — and that is not very pragmatic!

Chairperson: Thank you, Vikram. We're going to start what we call the response and challenge round, or the challenge round. I'd like to invite the first person from the proposing team to issue the challenge. Kishore, you have one minute.

Kishore Mahbubani: Thank you, Vikram. I am glad you said that pragmatism is like motherhood. So please do not vote against your mother in the final round. You said that we should have balanced pragmatism with morality and with idealism, implying that they sort of exclude each other. But you know, Mr S Rajaratnam said many years ago — and I quote — "Unsentimental pragmatism has made life more human, more dignified, and more hopeful for Singaporeans". So what could be more moral and more idealistic than what Mr Rajaratnam has spelt out?

Chairperson: Eugene, I need you to respond to that question from Kishore.

Eugene Tan: I think it's important to recognise that when we talk about pragmatism here, we are concerned about pragmatism being elevated to a point where we do not consider other imperatives. So putting it another way, it is not just about getting to the summit of the mountain but fundamentally about *how* we get to the summit. Are we going to leave people behind in that pursuit? We should not underestimate the importance of morality, principles and values. The shared purpose will always be there, but how do we discipline that shared purpose? We take the view that pragmatism alone is not enough; if anything; unbridled pragmatism will get us into a lot of trouble.

This is where we are coming from, and we need to recognise the imperative for pragmatism to be balanced. We are not saying do away with pragmatism. We are saying that we need to be even-handed. We need to be pragmatic but we also certainly need to look at concerns, particularly at this stage of our development where our material needs are more or less satisfied. We need to go beyond those material needs and engage the aspirations. How do we build a nation when everyone is driven by pragmatic considerations? How do we create a national soul? How do we get people to feel that this is a place where we will stay regardless of whether things are good or bad? We take the view that pragmatism alone will do us in. Pragmatism will get us through the day but we need more than pragmatism to get us through the night. As a society, we need to go beyond material concerns to incorporating post-material aspirations as well.

Chairperson: Thank you. Now you have a minute to issue a challenge to the proposing team.

Eugene Tan: The Proposition has presented pragmatism as something workable. Vikram and I do not disagree with that. But isn't pragmatism ultimately ideological? That, in the end, pragmatism will actually kill any discussion as it prevents us from looking at alternatives. Well, because what is pragmatic is the path we take. It tells us to focus solely on what works. But it does not tell us how it works, how we are going to get there. So the question for the Proposition is: How are we going to build a nation? If we have people who treat this place like a hotel, people will say, "Well, it does not make sense for me to stay here any longer. I might as well get up and go". Then the past 50 years would have been a waste. Thank you.

Chairperson: Thank you. Tong Yee, you are going to respond. You have two minutes starting from now.

Tong Yee: I think one of the things that amazes me most is that and this goes with my experience — I have just come from one of our ITEs [Institutes of Technical Education], that is ITE Central, and I remember while growing up in Singapore, I wondered why Singapore did not have a sense of equality or justice and why we stereotyped one group over another. But stepping into that ITE campus earlier, I met youths speaking to me with confidence and dignity. I am proud of the fact that we have, our country has, built such a facility. And I would say that the ITE itself is idealism. It is idealism to create equal education for all. But I do remember that it took us some time to get there. So when we are pragmatic, we begin to build things. I really think that it is a question of time and that in time itself you will begin to see that with a foundation of pragmatism, you eventually will be able to fulfil, I guess, all the idealisms that we do stand for as a nation.

Chairperson: You have another forty-seven seconds if you want to continue before you challenge.

Tong Yee: I don't have anything else to say.

Chairperson: If not, carry on issuing the challenge to the opposing team now.

Kishore Mahbubani: Thank you. The most surprising thing you said was that pragmatism, at the end of the day, is an ideology. As far as I know, that is a contradiction. An ideological approach is the opposite of a pragmatic one, if you follow what ideology says and what pragmatism says. It was John Kenneth Galbraith who said, "I react pragmatically. Where the market works, I'm for that; where the government is necessary, I'm for that. I'm deeply suspicious of somebody who says I'm in favour of privatisation or in favour of government". That is ideology. How can you confuse ideology with pragmatism?

Chairperson: Thank you, Kishore.

Vikram Khanna: I will speak on behalf of Eugene. I think, just to clarify, that an ideology is when somebody says pragmatism alone should be a governing principle, pragmatism and nothing else. That has the effect of elevating pragmatism to the level of an ideology. And I think that's a fair statement to make.

Chairperson: Eugene, would you like to respond as well? You have more time.

Eugene Tan: Since Professor Kishore Mahbubani quoted an economist, let me quote an economist in return. Douglass North said that strong moral and ethical codes of a society are the cement of social stability, which makes an economic system viable. In the end, it is important to look beyond pragmatism that is required in a given situation. What is it that we hope to get out of a certain policy? You said that pragmatism is not an ideology. But I would submit that it is an ideology simply because it tells you how to go about doing things, working on a basis of what works.

Chairperson: You now have some time to issue a challenge to the proposition team.

Vikram Khanna: Kishore, I will be a little kinder to you than you were to us. As you are a foreign policy expert, I will ask you a question on foreign policy. Singapore supported the Iraq war, which was a violation of international law and also a violation of the UN Charter. Was that pragmatic? And was that right?

Kishore Mahbubani: I must say that is an excellent question. The simple answer is that it was a good, pragmatic decision on the part of Singapore to support the Iraq war. Because if you look at the foreign policy alternatives that Singapore had at that time — what choices it had and what it had to do — it was clear that, on balance, it was better for Singapore to support the Iraq war. Many of you probably do not know about the remarkable amount of benefits that Singapore has gained as a result of that decision.

As a result of the goodwill that we built up in Washington, DC, we developed a much closer defence relationship with the United States. As a result of building up a closer defence relationship with the US, we expanded the geopolitical space for Singapore, and we have much more freedom of action than a small state can have on its own. And as we look ahead and as we think about how we defend ourselves in the long term, it pays to have this close defence relationship with the US. I can tell you that small states that ignore geopolitical realities, and assume that they can just take a moral stand and get away with it, are the states that get into trouble in the long run.

Chairperson: Ladies and gentlemen, I will now invite you to vote again to see whether or not your views have changed, by the other side particularly the Opposition, to change your mind. The motion is "Pragmatism should be retained as Singapore's governing philosophy". Those of you who agree, please press "1", those of you who disagree, please press "2".

2ND VOTING RESULT:
PROPOSITION — 56.4%, OPPOSITION — 43.6%

Chairperson: And we have your answers. Well done to the Opposition, very interesting. And we will open the floor to questions and see whether or not you manage to tilt the balance again. But before I do that, I will ask each team a question. For the Proposition, I would like to ask: Is pragmatism a philosophy or is it merely a means to an end?

Kishore Mahbubani: Pragmatism is actually a very deep philosophy that goes back a long, long time. There is even a school of philosophy called pragmatism. Over time, humanity accumulates wisdom. And as part of that wisdom, in order to succeed, to be able to deliver a good life for their citizens, to be able to ensure that people can escape wars, societies have developed this philosophy of pragmatism. If it were just a means to an end, then presumably you would say that anything goes. But I think you will notice that most of the philosophers who have argued in favour of pragmatism suggest that if your goal is to create a better life for your people, if your goal at the end of the day is to ensure that people are better off rather than worse off, then you should move towards pragmatism. And you will find roots of pragmatism in all of the great cultures in the world, not just in Western philosophy. You will find it in Indian philosophy and in Chinese philosophy. So it's something that is found all over the world, and the fact that it has existed in all cultures for such a long period of time suggests that it is a philosophy and not just a means to an end.

Chairperson: Thank you and now to the Opposition. Surely pragmatism remains important for the success of Singapore in the long run. How would you rate it compared to the other values and ideals that you think the government should consider in how it governs Singapore?

Eugene Tan: Certainly, pragmatism is important. I spoke earlier about the need for us to be even-handed — looking at what pragmatic considerations, what sort of moral objectives and what sort of aspirational concerns we can address. Let me give you an example. We all talk about how globalisation has enabled Singapore to prosper. But we also know that globalisation does not lift all boats to the same level. For a long time, we have worked on the premise that most people have benefitted from globalisation. This utilitarian perspective has worked very well for us. It is easy to justify as a matter of public policy. But things have changed. So now we have the Workfare Income Supplement. It is an attempt to recognise that economic globalisation does not benefit everyone. But as a society, we cannot just leave these people by the wayside. There is a need to try to help them level up. You can see the pragmatic consideration of wanting to be open to globalisation. But there is also the recognition that we need to be more than pragmatic. Madam Chair, it's not about preferring one over the other. It is really about being even-handed.

Chairperson: Vikram, would you like to add to that?

Vikram Khanna: We are not against pragmatism. Like I said, it is like motherhood. Nobody is against it. The problem is if you want to make it the sole ruling philosophy.

Chairperson: Or the most important ruling philosophy.

Vikram Khanna: No, that is not what the motion says. The motion says pragmatism should be the governing philosophy.

Chairperson: So are we now having a discussion on the motion?

Vikram Khanna: No, I do not want to be too technical. I mean, we also need a moral compass. We need principles. We need things that, as the Prime Minister said, are unshakeable. We don't have the rule of law because it's pragmatic. We have rule of law because it's intrinsically good in and of itself. We don't have meritocracy or interethnic harmony because it's pragmatic. It is good. I think we must have things that are intrinsically good in and of themselves whether they are pragmatic or not. I think that's the difference.

Chairperson: Thank you, Vikram. I'd like to now open the floor to questions. If you'd like to pose it to a particular member of the team, please let us know. Anybody? The gentleman over there in blue. Please identify yourself when you get to the microphone and whether or not you are opening the question to everyone, a team or to specific people.

Question 1: I'm Jared. My question is for all the speakers. We were talking about philosophy so I thought I'd take a page from Plato's *The Republic* and ask this. Pragmatism is a governing philosophy and it applies not just to states but perhaps to people too. You might say people have governing philosophies. So it seems to me that somebody whose governing philosophy is pragmatism might not be a very good person. As a child, I don't want my mum to be pragmatic to me. I want her to love me even though she might not get a good cost benefit return. I want her to love me even though she might take reputational damage. It should never be that kind of pragmatic consideration. And so, people should not always be pragmatic. So maybe we want to think that states also should not always be pragmatic, at least as a kind of governing philosophy. Does that sound right or is there some problem with the analogy between people and states? Or where have I gone wrong?

Chairperson: Jared, are you posing that question to anybody in particular?

Vikram Khanna: I will volunteer to answer. I think that is a very interesting question. I think it is true that pragmatism can also become a personal belief system. I do not know if you have seen the movie *Whatever Works* by Woody Allen. It is a fantastic movie. Let me summarise the plot. It is about a 70-something-year-old guy in New York called Boris Yellnikoff who has a very bleak view of life. He decides that he should just do whatever works to make him happy. And then every character in the film has the same philosophy. They just do whatever works. And so Boris gets married to a woman 50 years younger than he is and then divorces her. Her parents, who are from the south of the US and very religious, come to New York to rescue their daughter from this dirty old man. The mother, who is a strict Christian, decides to become an avant-garde photographer and has multiple boyfriends. The father, who is also religious, discovers that he is gay and that he can have a gay life in New York and so on. This is a comedy of course, this is Woody Allen, but I think it is very illustrative of what can happen when people adopt a philosophy of "whatever works" in their personal lives.

There is a guru of personal pragmatism in China called Ding Yuan Zhi who wrote a book called *Square and Round*. It offers pragmatic advice on how to live your life and there are some very interesting tips. For example, he says to show indifference to another person, release your handshake immediately on contact. If you want to make advances towards a certain lady, you should take advantage when she is sick; doing so will surely be effective because she will be weak and most in need of comfort. If you want to buy cheap clothes, ask the price of expensive clothes first. If you have a small request, first make a large request. Then let the other person refuse. When he feels apologetic, that is when you make your small request. So this is a pragmatic guru, his book is a perversion of an American self-help book.

Now this is the sort of behaviour that you will get when people make pragmatism a personal belief system and I think that is dangerous. I think it can happen. Most people are not like that. Most people believe in principles, in morality. And most people have a moral compass. So when you appeal to people, you have to show those qualities. You cannot say I am doing this because it's pragmatic. You sometimes have to say I am doing this because it is right.

Chairperson: Thank you, Vikram. Would anybody like to respond or say anything?

Tong Yee: I have two quick responses to this. First, I want to make sure that we do not detract from the motion here — it is about pragmatism being our governing philosophy. I think every single individual has every right to be whatever they choose to be and I have every right to be idealistic and I really am. I find it weird that I myself am sitting on this particular side of the debate. Second, we are not against what the Opposition is saying. You are saying that there needs to be some sort of balance and I absolutely get it. But the question is really whether pragmatism should be the governing philosophy.

Kishore Mahbubani: I must say that I love the story by Woody Allen. One of the great things about living in New York was the ability to watch a lot of Woody Allen movies. And people watch them and enjoy them; but to the best of my knowledge, very few people replicate what they see in Woody Allen movies in their personal lives. Also, that is not what this debate is about. It is not about what you do in your personal life. I would certainly agree that in your personal life, the most important and fundamental thing is to be moral and ethical and to do the right thing. That is the case in your personal life. But remember that nation states are different from human beings.

The tragedy of history — and there are five thousand years of human history you can go back and refer to — shows us that when states, especially small states, begin to behave like priests and saints, they end up in deep trouble. So that is not what we are debating today. We are not debating what you should do with your personal life. I completely support the Opposition when they say that we should not be pragmatic in our personal lives. But that is not what the debate is about. The debate is about what states should do and, more importantly, what small states should do. And when you come to the final round of voting, I hope you will remember that you are voting about states and not human beings.

Tong Yee: Let me put it this way. When I first chose to participate in this debate, I asked myself a question: "Why on earth would I agree to something insane?" I love Singapore deeply and I am very proud of it. And I am not in a position to say that I am proud of Singapore because we have been completely pragmatic. I think it has been a sound, realistic philosophy and, at the same time, we have been courageous. We have been bold and when we look at what we are debating about, I think we have something to be proud of. And I don't think that feeling of pride comes completely from a Machiavellian utilitarian approach. Singapore has balanced itself as well as we can. And as far as the state is concerned, yes, we have pragmatism as our governing philosophy. I don't think that we have lost all those other ideals or values that make us stand out as a very small and very proud nation.

Vikram Khanna: Kishore, I agree that we are talking about states and not about personal behaviour. We are only answering the gentleman's question. He asked about personal behaviour. That said, I do not think it is irrelevant. I think if a state exhibits 100 per cent pragmatism in everything it does, it can influence people's personal behaviour. It should not, but it can and it does in some cases.

Chairperson: Okay, I'd like to take back control of the debate and open it back to the floor. Are there any other questions? Yes, please.

Question 2: My question is directed at the Opposition. If I may suggest, if pragmatism is not to be our governing philosophy, then presumably the corollary to that is that ideology should be our governing philosophy. So let me posit you the case of Charlie Hebdo. Freedom of speech is an ideology. If ideology is to be a governing philosophy, then you should have complete freedom of speech under any circumstance. That is numero uno but then you wind up with Charlie Hebdo. A pragmatic view would say freedom of speech is a good thing but we need to temper it with what is practical and what is appropriate for society at large. And then you would say, maybe you would want to temper that ideology with a sense of what is real and practical in a multiracial society. So in that context do you really think that ideology should really trump pragmatism?

Vikram Khanna: I do not think we ever said we should throw out pragmatism and substitute it with ideology. Pragmatism must be there. Pragmatism should be an element of any governing philosophy. But it is not the whole thing, that is the point. The motion says pragmatism should be the governing philosophy, not a philosophy should be tempered by pragmatism. So I totally agree with you, you cannot take a black-and-white ideological view of the Charlie Hebdo issue.

But this is not just an issue of pragmatism versus ideology. It is also about values. Unbridled free speech is one of France's core values. In our case, free speech does not extend to having the freedom to insult someone's religion. We take this position not merely out of pragmatism, but because we believe it to be right in itself.

Eugene Tan: Do not be blindsided. Like it or not, pragmatism as it is practised in Singapore can operate, and does operate, as a form of ideology. It says let us focus on what works; it does not matter how we are going to get there. We

137

should not be fooled by the Proposition's view that we are proposing an ideological stand. There will always be competing ideologies. What is important is that we have to be even-handed. Freedom of speech is as important in our society as the right of people to not be offended, particularly when it comes to their religious beliefs. And we are not saying that we should sacrifice one for the other. It is really approaching it in a contextual manner. So the text, take the Constitution for example, operates in a context. It's important to recognise that.

Chairperson: Thank you, Eugene. Would you like to say anything, Kishore?

Kishore Mahbubani: I think I understand why they got more votes in the second round. They seem to be agreeing with us more and more. I know that they are in a difficult position as they are arguing against motherhood but, you know, they are going all over the place. You either say that pragmatism should be retained as our governing philosophy or you say it should be dropped. The Opposition should be arguing that pragmatism should be dropped, but they are not doing so.

Chairperson: Thank you. The gentleman at the back, if you could just give us your name.

Question 3: I am Paul Tambyah from the medical school. My question is directed at Professor Mahbubani. You quoted Mr Rajaratnam. I would like to give you another quote from Mr Rajaratnam, who was famously quoted as saying Singaporeans should not become people who know the price of everything and the value of nothing. And, in fact, if you think about it, 50 years ago, we had world champion badminton players, we had a hockey team that went to the Olympics and did not get thrashed 16–1 by Malaysia, we had the centre of the Malay film industry and we had a dynamic rock 'n' roll culture. But all of those things were rejected because they were not pragmatic, because they did not help deal with the basic needs of Singapore society, which were housing, medical care and other development imperatives. As a result of which, we had to jettison our sporting and cultural icons at the altar of pragmatism.

So my question is when it comes to an issue like sovereignty, which we discussed in the morning, do we really have to sacrifice our principles in support of what our current American president calls a dumb war, a rash war, just so that we can achieve a certain amount of limited goals? I really believe — in line with what the Opposition is saying — that pragmatism itself has got very limited benefits. It is going to help you in the short term, it is going to help you achieve goals A and B. But if you want to have long-lasting goals, you need something bigger, better than that, and I think the audience here has gone from 73 to 56 and at the next step, they will vote for the Opposition. Thank you.

Kishore Mahbubani: I wish we had a supporter in the audience as strong as that! Three quick points. First, I completely agree with Mr Rajaratnam on what he said about individuals. It is wrong for individuals to know the price of everything and not the value of anything. And that is why I emphasised that, for individual behaviour, the most important thing is to be moral; I completely agree with Mr Rajaratnam there. I could not quite follow your second point about us losing the cultural icons because there is an echo effect up here (*on stage*). But let me emphasise that not all of the decisions that Singapore has made in the last 50 years have been correct. Like any other society, Singapore has made mistakes. To give you a large and obvious example, in our rush to develop and modernise, we did not preserve neighbourhoods like Chinatown. Beautiful old districts were torn down. But that was the price we paid for rapid development in the early days. So we made mistakes. The critical point is: if you are pragmatic, you learn from your mistakes; and that is what Singapore has been doing over the years. Now, finally, your point about the Iraq war. You are right. There are people who are opposed to it, and there are good reasons for opposing it. But the question is: what should Singapore, as a small state, do?

Chairperson: Thank you. Would either of you like to respond to that? If not, we'll open the floor to questions again.

Question 4: My name is Rahul and my question is for the Opposition. You are essentially arguing that pragmatism should not be our governing philosophy.

So then the question is, what should our governing philosophies be? I know you mentioned values and ideals but could you give specifics?

Vikram Khanna: I think I have mentioned in my brief remarks that we should have a pragmatic approach to our governing philosophy. That is completely different from saying pragmatism should be our governing philosophy. A pragmatic approach would include elements of pragmatism. Of course there are times when we have to be pragmatic. There are times when we also have to be moral. There are times when we have to take a stand on what is right and wrong. There are times when we have to have things that are unshakeable, things that have to be done whether they are pragmatic or not.

We have mentioned the rule of law, interethnic harmony and meritocracy. There are societies that have ditched these things. There are societies that have ditched the rule of law. The rule of law has become the rule of man, or some men. There are societies that do not practise tolerance towards all religions. There are also societies that practise ethnic majoritarianism. They do these things because they think it is pragmatic for them. That is not what Singapore should do. It would go against our core values. These values are part of our governing philosophy. So there are many elements of what our governing philosophy should contain. Pragmatism is one of them and only one of them.

Chairperson: Is there another question from the floor?

Question 5: My question to the Proposition is this. Could you please explain to Singapore citizens what the pragmatic value of the national pledge is? Because the layman on the street does not deeply believe that idealism should be the governing philosophy of the government. However, we need to implement idealism in a pragmatic way rather than the other way round. So I deeply believe that idealism should be our governing philosophy. Otherwise, if I propose to you, let us abolish the national pledge — because what is the pragmatic value for the layman on the street to recite the national pledge every National Day?

Chairperson: So the question is what is the practical purpose of reciting the pledge? What is the purpose of having a pledge?

Tong Yee: For me, it is entirely tied to context. If you are dealing with a multicultural and multireligious young nation, I think the national pledge is one of the most pragmatic things you will ever see. It talks about equal opportunity, it talks about the fact that we treat all people equal, and although a one nation itself is an ideal, it is pushing for a certain ideal. It is very pragmatic.

Chairperson: Over there, gentleman in the blue shirt.

Question 6: My name is Osman from Pertapis. Actually, I felt very connected with Professor Eugene Tan when he talked about the even-handed approach. To be seen as a caring government, the pragmatic approach is one good thing. But on the flipside, you could also be seen to adopt excessive or even extreme measures to achieve your pragmatic policies. So in 500 BC, Aristotelian ethics recommended the golden mean, which is prevalent in Islam, Christianity and Buddhism, where, for any policy, you have to take the middle mean between the extremes so that you will develop a caring and sharing society where nobody is left out. But if you keep on pursuing a very pragmatic approach on the flipside, you might be likely to be seen as oppressive or even sidelining certain communities or certain issues that are important to the minorities. I suggest that we adopt a pragmatic golden mean approach. What do you say, Professor Tan?

Chairperson: Professor Tan, please.

Eugene Tan: Thank you, Osman, for your support! Hopefully you can persuade people on your table to support us as well. I emphasised earlier the importance of being even-handed. We are not suggesting that we replace one ideology with another. But as society matures, we need to go beyond being pragmatic. It does not mean that pragmatism is thrown out of the window. It just means that pragmatism will now have to co-exist with other equally important things. Had we been pragmatic, well, we might as well not have the national pledge. The pledge exhorts us to do many things, and I think the Proposition has, in many ways, acknowledged the importance of not being pragmatic but to hold ourselves to a higher standard, to bring ourselves to a higher level. Is it "pragmatic" to do away with minorities? One could say that. I have students who have said that we should have an all-Chinese workforce in a company because it would be much easier to not have to cater for *halal* food during company events and the employees could all speak in Chinese or the same dialect. But is that what we want? Because this is what pragmatism will ultimately lead us to. We have got to go beyond that, recognising that pragmatism is essentially going for whatever works. It is important; we do not deny that. But we need to rise above that and recognise that we shouldn't be enslaved by pragmatism. Ultimately, we should ask ourselves, what is the point of Singapore being here? We might as well not exist at all *if* that is the "pragmatic" thing to do.

Chairperson: Does either of you have anything to say to him?

Kishore Mahbubani: I am somewhat confused by the arguments of the Opposition. The key line you used, Eugene, is that as society matures, we need to go beyond pragmatism. But go where? What is unclear about your argument is: where are you taking us? I know you keep saying that we should become more moral and choose ideals, but are you actually advocating that we abandon pragmatism? And if you are saying that we are not abandoning pragmatism, then aren't you agreeing with us? So what I am trying to say is, what are you disagreeing with? Are you saying that Singapore should drop pragmatism as its governing philosophy? And if we drop it, where do we go, what is your destination and where are you taking us?

Chairperson: You have to respond.

Eugene Tan: Thanks for the extra airtime. We certainly take the view that pragmatism must remain part of the governing philosophy. We recognise the importance that pragmatism plays in public policy having to deal with finite resources. But we need to go beyond that. We need to go beyond pragmatism because society demands more and it is also the right thing to do. If we say that we should do away with the poor, with minorities, on one level, it can be seen as pragmatic. On another level, it would go against what Singapore actually represents. Professor Kishore Mahbubani has been trying to press us to say what would come in place of pragmatism. We have offered the perspective that we should be even-handed. We should now have the even-handed approach, balancing pragmatism with what it means to be Singaporean, what it means to be in Singapore. What does our society stand for? I think that's important. If we want to have a soul as a nation, we need to go beyond cost-benefit analysis.

Kishore Mahbubani: Let me state an important historical fact which is important for us to take on board during this debate. The British left behind multiracial colonies in all parts of the world: Guyana in South America, Cyprus in Europe, Sri Lanka in South Asia, Singapore in South-east Asia and Fiji in the Pacific. If you look at this list of five, four out of the five failed to manage their ethnic relationships because the societies were not pragmatic. They took an ideological position, which then led to disaster. So if your concern is, say, ethnic harmony and making sure we all stay together, I suggest that you go and study these cases of the former British colonies, and study why they failed. The fundamental reason why they failed is because they were not pragmatic. So if your goal is to ensure that, then the rest should learn from Singapore.

Eugene Tan: I think Professor Mahbubani failed to mention that the British left behind a dominant race in all these other countries. We chose not to take that "pragmatic" path. The British decided in Malaya, in Sri Lanka, to have a dominant group. We decided to go against that and that has made all the difference. Because we chose not to be pragmatic, we chose to treat the minorities with sensitivity, short of affirmative action.

Chairperson: Would anybody else like to ask a question? Gillian, please.

Question 7: May I invite the speakers to engage in very specific policy issues. First, a choice was made to license two integrated resorts. Was that a pragmatic decision for job creation and do you stand against that? Another policy decision is that we made a choice to institute CPF [Central Provident Fund], which is to beat our human instincts not to plan for the future and force us to set aside money for retirement. Is that a pragmatic choice? Was it unwise? Third, we made a practical choice to institute GRCs [Group Representative Constituencies]. It is a basic minimum guarantee that minorities will have representation in parliament. Was that a pragmatic or incorrect choice? Finally, the government constantly makes the choice to have public consultation in-between general elections. It is a pragmatic and practical choice to engage as many people as possible as they make their policy choices. Is that a pragmatic choice but an incorrect and wrong one? So can the motion "the conference resolves that pragmatism remains important and should be retained as our government philosophy" be turned down?

Chairperson: Thank you, Gillian, for the four questions. I suggest we take them by theme. The first question was on the integrated resorts, the second was on CPF and choice, the third was on GRCs and the fourth on if it is correct for the government to have public consultation between general elections to engage as many people as possible in the last fifty years? So there were four questions in Gillian's one question. Would you all like to take all four at one go or I suggest we take it topic by topic. Can I suggest that we take the issue of the integrated resorts and the decision on the integrated resorts? Could I ask the Proposition to take that on first?

Tong Yee: Kishore is going to kill me for this one. If there is one thing that I can't do, it is speak against what I genuinely believe in. I understand the reasons why we opened the integrated resorts but that was something that we chose based on our pragmatic reasons and I personally am against them. I get that we have a prettier skyline right now but, in the social sector, we are dealing with a lot of people who have not benefitted from this. So personally, I would lean towards the other end. I really want to present it as an idea itself, that this is really perhaps one of the exceptional things that we did, but I think that it is still being debated.

Chairperson: So the Proposition would have rejected its own motion in this case because he does not believe that the government made a correct choice there?

Kishore Mahbubani: No, hang on. I think you have misstated what Tong Yee is trying to say. We did say earlier that the government has made mistakes in the process of pragmatism, and you can argue that the casinos were a big mistake. Frankly, in my case, to be completely blunt and honest with all of you, my father went to jail because of gambling debts. My family suffered because of gambling. So if you were to ask me if I would vote for casinos, my answer is no.

Chairperson: Would the Opposition like to take on that issue?

Vikram Khanna: I would concede yes. I think having casinos was a pragmatic decision: it is a job creator, it adds another engine to the economy and tourism, and it has been a success. While there have been problems and cases of problem gambling, there are safeguards to prevent that and I think the social fallout has not been that bad. So it was totally a pragmatic decision and I have no problem with it.

Eugene Tan: I think we have forgotten who the Proposition is and who the Opposition is! The IRs were a pragmatic decision. That is where many of us have difficulty because we feel that it goes against certain things that we believe in. Have we become bankrupt of ideas such that we need to have the IRs? Having said that, I think it's also important to recognise that we are also trying to square the circle. Singapore opted for the IRs for whatever pragmatic and economic considerations but we are also trying to see how we can create a virtue out of a vice. How can we come out with new forms of regulation that will ensure that the casinos and the IRs actually work for us? To some extent, we have done so. But there will always be that constant tension. This constant tension will help public policy to be better. If we had just been solely pragmatic, we would not have bothered about the social fallout that would have arisen from the introduction of casino gaming in Singapore. So I hope that sets clear that we are the Opposition!

Chairperson: In the interest of time, I'm going to focus on the next question regarding GRCs before we have the closing arguments. So if I could ask the Proposition to take on the issue of GRCs.

Kishore Mahbubani: Actually, I am glad Gillian asked the question about GRCs because I want to emphasise that the word "our", in this case, refers to Singapore as a society and not the ruling party. So we do not have to argue in favour of what the ruling party does. The GRCs were a decision made by a political party, and not necessarily a decision by Singapore as a society.

Eugene Tan: This is where Professor Mahbubani has revealed the soft underbelly of pragmatism. We are not clear, in the end, to what ends, or rather who, does pragmatism serve. Sometimes, we are not clear whether it even serves the people. Sometimes, we are not clear whether it serves the government and, sometimes, we are not clear whether it serves the state. Looking at Professor Mahbubani's response, it is clear that there are difficulties with pragmatism as it is practised because it could easily be used to further the ends of the ruling party. It could certainly be used to further the ends of society. So what I am saying is that this is a very fungible concept. It is as much an ideology that enables the ruling party — the government — to use it, and to say that it works for society and that is why we should have it. So in response to Gillian, I would say that the GRC scheme was a pragmatic response to the government's claim then that people were voting along racial lines. But I see also the idealism that is also vested in it. The idealism is to have the political parties behave in a moderate manner. In order to win votes, they need to pool votes from the different racial groups. That represents both a pragmatic response as well as an idealistic response. As I tell students in my constitutional law class, let's look at the policies, the institutions for what they are worth. Let us, for the moment, put aside how the ruling party uses it to its advantage. But it still raises the real possibility that pragmatism can be misused.

Chairperson: Thank you. Vikram?

Vikram Khanna: Just to add to the point of pragmatism for whom. I think the issue that Eugene has mentioned is very important. There are many questions here where it is not clear. I mean you might say yes, it should be pragmatism for society. But let me give you two small concrete examples. Singapore has the highest acreage of golf courses among any country in the world. Who is this pragmatic for? Who does it work for? If all Singaporeans were golfers, I would say yes, build more golf courses. But I think if 2 per cent are golfers, who does it work for? Another thing, this goes back to history a little bit. We incarcerated many artists and playwrights in the 1970s. We had Operation Spectrum in 1987 when more people were incarcerated. This served to stifle artistic and cultural expression. Was this pragmatic? Who was this pragmatic for? Was it pragmatic for society? I am not going to answer this question. I will leave it to you to decide. So there are a lot of things that we have done which are of questionable value and I would not say they were quite so pragmatic.

Chairperson: I'd like to now invite the teams to make their closing arguments. For the Opposition, Eugene please, if you can take the standing microphone. You have five minutes.

Eugene Tan: Madam Chair, ladies and gentlemen, the Proposition has tried to paint Vikram and me as the high priests of idealism. Far from it. I would put it to you that there would have been no Singapore of today had pragmatism not prevailed in 1965. We would have simply keeled over and adopted the different courses that Mr Janadas Devan outlined earlier. My team's stand is that pragmatism remains undoubtedly important. What we have tried to do is to show how even in the different policies that may have come across as being pragmatic, idealism, values and principles have been nurtured in them as well. Being pragmatic is a given. But we must learn to leaven it even more. Pragmatism, because it focuses on what works, would also mean that we forget that we do have choices, even if they are difficult choices. It is important, as we move ahead, that we recognise that we do have a choice.

Pragmatism, unfortunately, tends to curtail any discussion because it gets people to focus only on whatever works. Pragmatism would be wholly inadequate in our next lap. In fact, it would probably be the recipe for our downfall. As I said earlier, it can get us through the day but we need more than pragmatism to get us through the night. In his book *Drive*, Daniel Pink reminds us of how motivation is intrinsically powered, comprising three elements: autonomy, which is the desire to be self-directed; mastery, which is the urge to be better, to excel; and third, purpose, the yearning to be part of something larger than ourselves.

As you can see, pragmatism will not enable us to rise above ourselves. It will suppress whatever autonomy we want because we will all have to worship at the altar of pragmatism. It will not encourage us to adopt a craftsman-like attitude, to attain mastery in whatever we do. Instead it will encourage us to go for what is expedient, what is convenient and to take short cuts. We must continue to have that sense of mission. But pragmatism enervates that very sense of mission.

Second, the Proposition has tried to paint the motion as being about society and not about individuals. But isn't it individuals who make up a society? And it is important here to recognise how the state's approach to many issues can ultimately affect how Singaporeans view policies. This is where it can be very problematic for nation-building in Singapore because pragmatism encourages citizens to take a very transactionary approach. What is in it for me? That results in the legitimacy of government policy being measured in pragmatic terms and, very often, that means in economic terms. That is why we now have this overwhelming preference for value rather than values.

Look at housing, for example. It is not only something that we think of, it is something that we think with. Think about how the Singaporean male has been caricatured. When he wants to get married to the lady he loves, he will say, "Let us go and apply for a HDB flat". It's all about using housing to think about these things.

Third, the Proposition asked where pragmatism would take us. I think it will enervate us of our ability to govern; it will take away the energy for collective action because we will tend to think about what works for us individually. So is it any surprise that, on economic matters, people are not really taking action in any meaningful way because they are constantly reminded that those are the issues that they are very worried about? It is easy to say that we do make mistakes and that pragmatism cannot be blamed. But it reminds us that pragmatism also consigns us into thinking only in terms of trade-offs. We need to go beyond trade-offs. So let me conclude: we do have a choice, and we should stop worshipping at the altar of pragmatism.

Chairperson: Thank you, Eugene. I'd like to now invite Kishore to present his closing remarks for the Proposition.

Kishore Mahbubani: My partner Tong Yee began by saying that as someone from the NGO world, it was a very unpragmatic decision on his part to come and argue in favour of pragmatism. I made an equally unpragmatic decision because I arrived this morning at 6am from Davos, where I fell ill, so you can see that I am slightly incapacitated in this debate. But when Janadas pushed me very hard to take this role, I actually agreed because it reflects a genuine and deep personal worry that I have about Singapore. I do worry when I hear Eugene say that it is time for us to go beyond pragmatism and weigh in other factors. There is a huge danger in his statement because there is one fundamental fact about Singapore that has not changed; that one fundamental fact is that we remain a small state. And fortunately, we have several thousand years of human history to go back and study in order to understand the state of small states. And clearly, the lessons of history teach us that when small states — and I must emphasise that we are talking about the state and not the government — stop being pragmatic, they get into deep trouble. I can predict three concrete examples of big challenges that are coming our way.

Number one is geopolitical. There is going to be an enormous geopolitical contest between the United States and China; I guarantee it. And if Singapore does not react carefully and pragmatically to this great geopolitical divide, we will suffer. Do not try to be moralistic in geopolitics if you are a small state because your head will be cut off. And that has not changed.

In the area of the economy, we know, even some of the leading developed states are struggling to cope with the new forces of globalisation. We have to change and adapt very quickly if we are going to make it, and if we stop being nimble and pragmatic, I assure you that Singapore will be washed away very quickly by another wave of global competition.

And finally, to refer to the internal area of society, which is what our opposition has focused on, we still remain a multiracial state. That has not changed. And I am glad that Piyush Gupta brought up the issue of the Charlie Hebdo affair. Because if you take the non-pragmatic approach, and you take the ideological approach that freedom of speech is everything that matters, Singapore is finished. As I was flying back this morning, I read an editorial in the *Economist* about the Charlie Hebdo affair that was pure rubbish. And if we follow that rubbish, we will suffer as a consequence. So as you can see, in all the big challenges that are coming our way, if we are to preserve Singapore as it is, we have to remain pragmatic. Now the key word that the Opposition used was "ideals". I suggest to all of you that the highest ideal that we as fellow Singaporeans can have is to try and preserve this small island city-state, which has a land territory that is so absurdly small that it is smaller than a small island in a lake in Sumatra. And on that tiny bit of territory, you are trying to create a complex city state that is competing with the rest of the world, that is trying to surpass the rest of the world, and if you forget that you have so few resources and so little territory, and you take idealistic and moral positions, as our opposition is suggesting, then sadly Singapore will be finished. So please, I beg you, retain pragmatism as our governing philosophy.

Chairperson: Thank you very much, Kishore. Thank you, ladies and gentlemen. And it's now my pleasure to invite all of you to see whether your minds have been changed again by our speakers and to take the last vote for the day. The poll says pragmatism should be retained as Singapore's governing philosophy. Those of you who agree, please press "1" and send it in. Those of you who disagree, press "2" and send it in. So one thing we all found in common is that Mr Janadas Devan had huge persuasive powers on all of us.

3RD VOTING RESULT:
PROPOSITION — 63%, OPPOSITION — 37%

The vote has swung back somewhat. Sixty-three per cent for the motion and 37 per cent against the motion. Congratulations to both teams. I believe many of you, I hope many of you, found this to be interesting, learnt something from today's discussion and debate, and found it scintillating. I would have liked to see somebody argue that the Singapore government is idealistic, is an ideological party and is formed as an ideological party but it is pragmatic in the way it delivered its policy to achieve those ideological outcomes which are meritocracy, multiracialism, nuclear family, subsidised healthcare and education. That's just one way we could have argued but thank you all very much. I hope you all have a good rest of the conference.

15

What if the Nation-State is No Longer the Key Organisational Unit of the International Community?

WANG GUNGWU

I do not believe in the end of history. It was surprising how quickly the nation-state came to be seen during the last few decades as the key organisational unit of the international community. I will not, however, be surprised if that ceases to be the case. The flux of historical change is the norm, but the idea of progress arising from scientific and technological advances does not apply to units of political organisation. No such unit has remained unchanged or unchallenged for long. It is justified to ask what other kinds of units could take the nation-state's place.

Janadas Devan, the Director of the Institute of Policy Studies, responds to one part of the question in the Preface of this book when he describes the very exceptional position of Singapore. His account of its origins — the difficult roads taken to enable Singapore to survive and grow — provides an excellent snapshot of how conditional and incalculable the fate of each unit that calls itself a "nation-state" can be. If the "city-state" of Singapore is a "nation-state" and an exceptional one, one may well ask, what is a "nation-state"?

THE MYTHS ABOUT THE ORIGINS OF THE NATION-STATE AND INTERNATIONAL LAW

My instincts as a historian are aroused because the city-state that Mr Devan describes is closer to what had been an ancient institution. There have been city-states of various kinds, and some did survive for centuries. They have not had a happy history and teach us nothing about the origins of nation-states.

On the other hand, nation-states are taken as the norm by many today who assume that such states have always been around. In fact, the nation-state is a very new idea. It came into being under a special set of circumstances in Western Europe.

Most of my colleagues, the political scientists in particular, would say that the system of nation-states dates from the end of the Thirty Years' War with the Peace of Westphalia of 1648. If that is correct, the nation-state can be said to have begun in one corner of the world over 300 years ago.

However, the more I learn about what happened before and after Westphalia, the more I am convinced that it is a myth that the nation-state began to play any historic role from the 17th century. The nation-state, as an organising unit of the international community, certainly cannot be dated back to the treaties signed at that time. Why do I say that?

The treaties signed at the time were not between nation-states but by more than a hundred Catholic and Protestant polities of many different jurisdictions and sizes that had been involved in religious wars for decades, some to a greater extent than others. The main protagonists that fought themselves to a standstill had decided that they should stop killing one another and sit down to talk about achieving a lasting peace "among good Christians". After several years of discussions, the various rulers finally agreed that they should draw up borders between the aggressive combatant states. Each of these sovereign states would agree not to interfere in the affairs of the others.

The treaties were, on the one hand, between kingdoms and empires and, on the other, between them and a large number of princely states, imperial cities and imperial bishoprics. There was no such thing as the nation-state in their eyes. What made the agreements enduring was the fact that they shared a deeply rooted cultural heritage, one based on a common religion and a respect for juridical authority. Nevertheless, there was one state that was close to becoming what we now recognise as a nation-state. This was the Dutch Republic that had fought the Eighty Years' War to gain its independence from the Spanish empire. Many historians acknowledge that this was the first state that established itself as a union of people with one language, one religion and a shared anti-imperial history.

The great innovation at Westphalia, nonetheless, was the idea that the sovereignty of each state should be respected and no state should interfere in the affairs of another. It has since been argued that it was this principle that enabled nation-states to emerge eventually. It is certainly true that some of the small princely states in Central Europe began to have safe borders, and some did survive for a long time. It should be clear though that these treaties, based on agreements reached among the powerful empires and kingdoms of the time, had little to do with the rising tide of nationalism later in the 19th century, which saw the formation of most of the European nation-states.

Westphalia represented a high point in the Age of Empires. By that time, the Spanish maritime empire was already powerful, and the Portuguese empire in Brazil, Africa and South and Southeast Asia was the most extensive, being spread around the world on all the known continents. Several decades earlier, the British, French and Dutch had launched merchant companies that began building their rival empires in the Americas and had then launched their commercial empires in Africa and Asia. Outside Western and Central Europe, there was the Russian empire in the north spreading eastwards overland into Central Asia and reaching beyond Siberia to the Amur River and the Pacific Ocean. Towards Central Europe, the Islamic Ottoman empire had probed deep into European lands and controlled the southern shores of the Mediterranean. Other inheritors of the Mongol empire had conquered most of the Indian Subcontinent. China under its Manchu Qing dynasty was feeling its way westwards to check the advances of the Turkic and Russian empires.

In short, the treaties at Westphalia agreed to largely by the rulers of empires, kingdoms and princely states in Western and Central Europe were to stop incessant fighting within Europe itself. This gave the smaller polities among them a period of relative peace and security that enabled some to develop their respective local identities ultimately into a sense of nationhood. They benefited from the fact that the expanding empires had agreed to pursue their imperial interests elsewhere. However, it is one thing to say that the idea of sovereignty began in the 17th century but quite misleading to say that was when nation-states came about.

The second myth is that it was an evolving system of international law that made the nation-state the organisational unit of the international community. Modern ideas of international law are said to date back to Hugo Grotius, following his 1625 treatise, a few decades before the Westphalia treaties. Grotius sought to establish a set of rules that would enable empires like those of the Portuguese and the Dutch to minimise their rivalry and warfare in Asia, especially in the maritime Malay world. His treatise was well-argued and what he proposed was necessary. This had nothing to do with the rise of nation-states though. It became necessary primarily because the Portuguese were Catholic and the Dutch were Protestant. Unlike earlier disputes between the Spanish and the Portuguese, both Catholic empires, the Protestant Dutch could not, like the Spanish earlier on, resolve their differences with the Portuguese by appealing to the Pope.

Thus, Grotius provided the two sets of Christian powers with the idea of drawing up a set of rules to minimise conflict. Of course, it did not stop the Dutch from seizing Malacca from the Portuguese in 1641 when they had the power to do so. When interests between empires collided, international law meant little. That was so then and threatens to remain true today.

Similarly, as efforts to draw up rules of peace and war developed, wars between empires continued over larger areas of the globe and with increasing ferocity. That reached a climax with the Napoleonic Wars which came to an end in the early part of the 19th century. One of its results was that the British naval empire in the East won out totally against that of the French. Ironically, this has been regarded as a high point in the evolution of international law, with the treaties associated with the Congress of Vienna that was convened in 1814 ensuring that a peaceful era for Europe would last for several decades.

The various meetings that accompanied the Congress did work out more permanent understandings as to what sovereignty might mean for empires and the Great Powers, and what the law could and should allow. International law could also affirm principles as to why states should not invade each other and how they should behave towards one another. Some people would argue that it was only with such a set of international laws that small states could feel secure; and only with the existence of such law could nation-states become a key unit in the international community.

That is an acceptable proposition but it must be clear that this happened because it was also in the interest of the powerful empires to agree to it. International law was not designed with nation-states in mind but was really about minimising conflict between very powerful European empires. These empires were then free to use their military power to expand their respective empires in the rest of the world. For example, with better understanding among them, they could carve out different parts of Asia and Africa without resorting to war among themselves.

In any case, the countries that really mattered were the Great Powers led by the British national empire and supported by the equally nationalist French empire. Other kinds of empires, like the Austro-Hungarian, the Prussian and the Tsarist Russian, were not far behind. By the 1840s, it was understood that the civilisation undergirding the law of nations was Christian and only civilised nations could be regarded as equal sovereign states. The Islamic Ottoman empire was admitted only after agreeing to extra-territorial rights in what might be described as an unequal treaty. Later, under military pressure and the threat of war, the Qing dynastic empire in China and the Buddhist Siamese empire submitted to similar conditions of what was described as international law. Soon afterwards, American show of "Black Ships" power in Tokyo Bay brought the Japanese emperor to accept a similar kind of unequal treaty.

It was also in this context that the Qing empire was forced to conform to the standards of civilisation dictated by Britain and France. By those standards, neither the Qing empire nor the Republic of China after 1912 was recognised as being "civilised". As long as the Chinese republic was regarded as weak and divided, it was not treated as an equal, full member of the international community. Only by accepting extra-territoriality was Qing China conditionally recognised by the other empires. By so doing, it also allowed a number of smaller European states to obtain Most Favoured Nation status that, when added together, subjected the treaty zones of China to becoming virtual parts of large and small Western Christian empires.

Perhaps the most significant shift in international law at the beginning of the 20th century was the equal status given to the Japanese empire after its surprising defeat of Qing China and later the Russian empire in the East. Clearly the acquisition of wealth and victories against other powers were the key criteria of civilisation even when Japan was not a Christian country. Yet, the Japanese could not overcome the issue of racial equality when the League of Nations met in Versailles in 1919. At the insistence of Britain, American President Woodrow Wilson as chairman denied Japan's proposal for the Japanese to be treated as equals. The Versailles meeting proved to be a rude awakening for both China and Japan, the former surrendering German rights in Shandong to Japan and the latter failing to gain racial equality for its people.

In short, the international law that was seen as maturing during the 19th century was not only about how empires should behave but also about which empires were more equal than others. It managed to reduce conflicts among national empires like those of the British and the French overseas but that did not stop them from expanding at the expense of other states. In the end, that law could not help the states avert the wars within Europe itself. As a result, two very destructive so-called World Wars followed each other closely. Ironically, the most destructive result of these two wars was not the demise of the small nation-states that were emerging in Central and Eastern Europe, but the collapse of the huge British and French empires.

It was only after 1945 that the world saw the age of the territorial empires finally come to an end. With global de-colonisation supported by a liberal, capitalist United States (US) as well as an internationalist Soviet Union (USSR), we can, for the first time, talk about the beginnings of a world of nation-states. With the United Nations (UN) replacing the League of Nations in 1945, the idea of using the nation-state as the key organisational unit for the rest of the world may be said to have become conceivable.

What made that feasible were two global developments. The first began in Europe with the secularisation of the Christian states during the 19th century. By the 20th century, it was possible for international law to accept that non-Christian states could also be treated as civilised. This enabled the Western powers to take the next step and consider the idea that former colonies might eventually qualify to become sovereign nation-states, all equal in law.

The second development followed the first. At the end of the Second World War, superpower rivalry was between enemies divided by secular and materialist ideologies — the US with its liberal capitalism and the USSR leading the charge for internationalist socialism. This led to a deadly struggle to draw all nation-states, especially the newborn post-colonial ones, into one camp or the other. Here, the small states must be thankful to international law, especially where it provided valuable cover for the new nation-states to be built and helped some of them resist the pressures of the two superpowers.

THE POST-SECOND WORLD WAR
LANDSCAPE OF THE NATION-STATE

I have turned to history to emphasise the fact that the nation-state became a key organisational unit for the world only very recently indeed. It was the UN that provided the structure which made that feasible. I recall how enthusiastic I was when I first learnt about its establishment in my final year at school in 1946. Later, at university, I was carried away by its promise and participated in the first meeting of the UN Students Association held in New Delhi in 1951. There, observing the new national pride of my fellow Indian students, I looked forward to the day when Malaya would become independent as a UN member state.

This was despite the fact that I felt disquiet that five countries were Permanent Members of Security Council and could act as super-states. When the UN rallied international forces to fight against invasion on the Korean peninsula in 1950, I was confident that we could count on the UN to ensure that small nation-states were safe from their big neighbours.

It turned out, however, not to be that simple. The Cold War led by the two superpowers lasted for more than four decades. When the USSR fell, the world was left with one superpower for some 25 years. The reality was that any powerful state could always find reasons to intervene in the affairs of smaller nation-states, not only in the new and poor ones in Africa and Asia but also in Eastern Europe.

In addition, the UN was helpless when some member-states were forcibly divided into two or more new states. We have seen how quickly Pakistan was divided into two. Then, the people of what could have been an obvious Korean nation-state have had to live ever since 1945 with what seems like an impossible dream. The unification of divided peoples has been possible but it was not something that the UN has enabled. At one end, we have the example of Vietnam reunified by a very bloody war that, unexpectedly, the US allowed the Vietnamese to win. At the other end, the reunification of Germany came about suddenly without any help from the UN.

It is in that context that we can see the reason for the "what if?" question that has been put to us.

I began by saying that Mr Devan rightly reminded us about the shifting borders around Malaysia that finally turned the parts of the British empire which use Malay as national language into three nation-states. For 20 years after the Second World War, there were no clear borders in most of this region. There has only been a more or less stable border since 1965. Singapore's neighbour had to fight very hard to make Indonesia the one country that it is today, not only against the Dutch who tried to hold on to parts of their empire but also against secessionist movements. Fortunately for Southeast Asia, all those efforts failed.

The survival of these states is not something that can, however, be taken for granted. The idea that once a nation-state gains its sovereignty anywhere, it will always be able to maintain it, has not been fully tested. The most glaring examples of how a "nation" can become several new nation-states can be seen from the collapse of the USSR, and the example that most surprised the whole world was the violent fragmentation of Yugoslavia. What kind of nation-state can turn into five different nation-states almost immediately after the death of its ruler?

That is a very cruel reminder that what is called the nation-state is still work-in-progress. There is hope that international law, the UN and all the institutions that the world has tried to support and strengthen for the last hundred years will succeed in protecting the nation-state ideal. The fact is there has been new thinking about global governance and about other kinds of organisational units to supplement or complement the nation-state.

ALTERNATIVES TO THE NATION-STATE

Is the nation-state the only organisational unit of the international community? Allow me to consider three other possible developments or arrangements. One is that some nation-states could set aside parts of their sovereignty and pool their resources to form larger unions, as has been the case with the European Union (EU). A second possibility is that some nation-states might opt to break up into more comfortable and sustainable units, for example, the Czech and Slovak republics and, possibly, also a future Scotland and Catalonia. A third possibility is a move away from nation-states altogether, with a group of city-states looking to the example of the once-flourishing Hanseatic League of Northern Europe as a model for that.

Let me assume that, given changing attitudes towards the global promise of the UN vision, the nation-state is no longer seen as the key organisational unit of the international community. Leading the way in this approach are states in Western and Central Europe where nation-states have had a longer history than anywhere else. Soon after the Second World War, some of them decided that they had enough of the conflict among them and began to plan for an EU. That was a bold vision that evoked for some, images of the Holy Roman empire but in modern form, and for others, it was something comparable to a federated United States of Europe. Here, ironically, it is the old notion of the European nation-state that now stands in the way of further development towards the kind of union their leaders are planning for.

Those who have observed the remarkable success of the Association of Southeast Asian Nations (ASEAN) would be keen to see that experiment go well too. The 10 member states are less ambitious than those in the EU. They are also more hopeful for ASEAN because most of them are still in the process of nation-building and not yet locked into deep national jealousies and fears. At the same time, because Southeast Asian polities are still developing to become nation-states, they are more sensitive about their respective sovereign rights. It is widely recognised that for them to have come this far is already an astonishing achievement, but it is not clear that with each member having only recently come to appreciate the need to build a nation-state, they will be prepared to move towards anything like a regional grouping comparable to a federal state.

The second arrangement or development is where people like the Scots, the Catalans and other ethnic communities contemplate the further division of their respective nation-states. They remind us that there are indeed many such groups in various parts of Asia and Africa that would be ready to follow their example and break away from "nation-states" that they no longer believe in. This would be an easy route to take if and when they find that their central administrations have become weak and divided, and other powers have declared that they have become "failed states". Also, should the breakaway efforts in Europe succeed, they could become the model for other groups. In particular, that would appeal to smaller ethnic groups in the socially pluralistic and less culturally integrated nation-states in the rest of the world. All of them would become vulnerable, not least those in Southeast Asia.

This Southeast Asian region is unlikely to forget what happened when the British denied India its full inheritance of the departing imperial power of "British India", and allowed the establishment of the separate Muslim state of Pakistan. That decision created an early example of "ethnic cleansing" and led to unceasing hostility along India's western borders. That was followed by the break-up of Pakistan into two and the creation of the state of Bangladesh. Closer to Singapore, the threat of secession in Aceh in Indonesia and the continual unrest in West Irian remind us that this region is not safe from border and regime changes.

Fortunately, the different national leaders around are still committed to the sacred task of building secure nation-states for their very complex mix of ethnic identities. It is unlikely that any of them will find secession of any kind acceptable but they will always have to ensure that there is enough wealth and power to manage the nation-state and keep the ideal afloat.

The third alternative arrangement to a world of nation-states for a Singapore that sees its future more as a global city than as a nation-state would be to look to the Hanseatic League example. It would, however, call for a great leap of the imagination to contemplate a future for a league of global city-states in today's world.

The Hanseatic League provided an effective zone of security over several centuries and was invaluable at a time when Europe did not have any structure of dependable order. There was nominally a single Holy Roman empire, but there was no authority that wielded enough power to enforce law and order over large swathes of territory. The League emerged to save the trading world of the Baltic and Northern Europe from piracy and anarchy, and was essential for mercantile survival under those conditions.

For cities and states like Singapore to contemplate anything like such an arrangement, there would have to be the expectation that the current international order might no longer be able to deal successfully with the protectionist impulses that threaten the global market economy. Such a league of cities could offer another layer of global governance. This could be developed within the current international order as long as the major powers agree to allow another channel for economic interdependence while political differences are being thrashed out among less friendly protagonists in another framework. Such city-state groupings need not replace the system of nation-states, but it could be an organisational unit that enhances the sense of global economic security when political and cultural conflicts prevail.

SOME SCENARIOS OF THE FUTURE GLOBAL ORDER AND HOME TRUTHS

Given the historical background and the possible alternatives to the nation-state, what I can offer are not answers to the question that has been posed but instead two scenarios of the global order and the future of nation-states, with comments on what seems likely and what seems not to be.

The first is: What if parts of the world decide not to deal with nation-states any further. Nation-states do not have to disappear but, should that happen, that would call for a world-state with the requisite power to control all states. That is most unlikely to succeed.

Assuming that nation-states survive but become dysfunctional or sub-servient to larger groupings, it is conceivable that two or more "imperial" states become powerful enough to divide the world. Each of them would organise bundles of subordinate partners (some, perhaps, called "allies") that do not insist on having sovereign "national" borders.

Under such conditions, it is possible for several regional (federal or con-federal) groups of "states" to be organised. Each of them would then be united by common security, economic and cultural interests.

In this scenario, there is nothing to prevent organisations based on allied cities (or city-states, all pluralist and non-national) from being formed. They could, together, construct strong networks, but always with the consent of the large "empires" and/or federated or confederated groups that agree that such network-leagues could also be useful in serving everybody else's interests.

The second scenario is a differently mixed system, with some nation-states holding on to their sovereignty. Such a global mix could consist of all or some of the following:

- Big states that seek to ensure they remain secure nation-states.
- Big states that are expansionist, building their own "imperial" networks.
- Small states that survive by being closely tied to larger economic or cultural "empires", retaining their sovereignty only in name.
- Small states that seek safety by forming (regional) federated or confederated units.
- City-states that offer to serve all the others equally.

Both scenarios would produce systems that cannot guarantee stability. There will always be some states ("imperial" or "federated") that will seek to change or improve upon the status quo to promote their own interests.

In summary, I am not sure we can say that the nation-state was ever the key organisational unit of the international community. It is an historic ideal and has served as a useful political and economic unit because powerful countries that are empires in everything but name had agreed to a set of rules by which smaller countries have been able to function. These powers will, from time to time, set out the key principles of interstate organisational behaviour, and these principles will prevail until the next re-configuration of powers is constituted.

During each period of broad agreement, big, medium and small countries will work out acceptable layers of relationships in order to attain relative peace all round. What is likely to remain is an international community grouped and re-grouped around a few big powers. Smaller states may have to be content to serve as the allies, partners, vassals or satellites of protective big powers. Some will do their utmost to avoid that fate and try not to become weaker, either by forming regional groupings of nation-states or by establishing networks of city-states. These groupings will find safety in numbers to achieve certain objectives, but each of them will still have to find their place in the framework of big power consent.

16

What if Singapore Has to Choose Between China and the United States?

JOSEPH LIOW

THE PRESENT GEOSTRATEGIC CONTEXT

With regard to what the present global and regional uncertainties portend for Singapore, the task of predicting the future is made more challenging by the difficulties involved in divining what the regional strategy of the United States (US) will look like under the presidency of Donald Trump.

Currently, America's Asia policy remains long on statements and short on substance. This may not be all that bad given the impression conveyed during the course of the Trump election campaign that the new president was intent on overturning the table on the prevailing global order and, closer to home, adopting an adversarial approach towards China. However, these are early days yet, and even though I have my doubts, it remains to be seen if President Trump would indeed translate his antagonistic views on China into actual policies.

Of course, the point can be made that the Trump administration's withdrawal from the trade pact across 12 countries, the Trans-Pacific Partnership (TPP), is a worrying portent. Indeed, this move — via President Trump's first presidential executive order no less — has thrown into serious doubt American interest in and commitment to the trade and economic agenda of the fastest-growing region in the world.

Yet we might wish to keep what has happened with the TPP in perspective and do that on at least three counts. First, the TPP is not quite dead yet.

Technically, to salvage the TPP, all that the remaining 11 signatories have to do is to commit to amending the enactment rules so that US participation is no longer required for the implementation of the deal. Of course, the absence of the US would dilute the significance, if not the value, of the agreement, but that is a different prospect to not having a TPP at all.

Second, the fate of American commitment to the TPP would have hung in the balance anyway under a new administration, regardless of who won the presidency. Lest we forget, almost all the presidential candidates on both sides of the divide, opposed the TPP. This included Hilary Clinton, the Democratic Party's candidate for the presidency, ironically an architect of the agreement. She may have been more amenable had she won, but she would not have reneged on a campaign promise. That would have meant that the TPP would have had to undergo fresh rounds of negotiation before the US was prepared to reconsider joining, let alone come on-board eventually.

Third, even if Trump has withdrawn the US by dint of a presidential executive order, there is every chance that a new administration further down the road might revive American interest in the TPP.

While 2016 was a watershed year for the US, 2017 will see significant political developments in China. This year will witness the leadership of the Chinese Communist Party (CCP) assemble for the 19th Party Congress. After a successful sixth Plenary Session of the CCP in October 2016 which saw the party rally around the "core leadership" of President Xi Jinping, it is widely expected that Xi will consolidate power by overseeing the appointment and retention of his key supporters and allies in the powerful Politburo Standing Committee. Although the prospects of any significant obstacle being placed before Xi appears remote at this point, consolidation may yet prove to be less straightforward than one might assume. For starters, given President Trump's penchant for off-the-cuff statements (and tweets), Xi will be cautious in his response to any Trumpian provocation on Sino-US relations. On one hand, Xi certainly cannot afford to appear weak in the face of any such provocation. Yet on the other hand, he would need to be careful not to over-stoke nationalist sentiments and hazard too strong a position in response lest such a move leads to an escalation that he is unable to walk away from without risking his own domestic credibility.

It is against this backdrop of uncertainty that the question arises: "What if Singapore has to choose between China and the US?" If you hope I will set out which of those powers Singapore should choose, then allow me to apologise from the very outset as I will disappoint you. This is because the matter of "choosing" is a deceptively simple way of approaching the complex problems that might confront us in the not-too-distant future.

The answer to such a question necessarily depends on a wide range of intervening variables and factors, such as what event or circumstances might prompt such a state of affairs, what sort of leadership resides in Washington, Beijing, or indeed, in Singapore at that particular point when a choice needs to be made, whether other regional states are confronted with the same dilemma, just to name a few. In other words, unless the scenario is fleshed out in sharper relief, it is difficult to answer this question in an informed manner. For that reason, perhaps what is more useful for us is to take a step back and look at this question in terms of its assumptions and implications. Before we consider the "what ifs", let us consider the "what was" or "what it used to be".

TAKING STOCK OF SOUTHEAST ASIA'S BALANCING ACT

It is fair to state, and there will be a consensus on this, that since the end of the Cold War, we have had a strategic equilibrium in East Asia that centred on stable Sino-US relations. That equilibrium allowed the region to flourish economically while at the same time kept the centrifugal forces of strategic competition very much at bay, or at least contained.

There are, now, concerns that things are in danger of unravelling and that we are on the cusp of change, not least with the inauguration of the Trump administration in the US. This is a deep anxiety that American interest and engagement in Southeast Asia are going to recede.

At the same time, China continues to be assertive in its foreign relations in the region and this will gather pace. There will obviously be positive elements in the form of its economic outreach especially through trade and investments into the region, but there is also another dimension to it which we have seen in recent times — what I would call political or diplomatic browbeating. China appears to have a fairly straightforward approach on this score: China is a great power and it expects deference from its neighbours for which it is prepared to reward them handsomely. Conversely, it need not countenance the recalcitrance of smaller states who refuse to accept this "fact" and all that it implies.

As for Singapore, our leaders have always stressed that the country works hard to ensure that we are not placed in a position where we have to choose between the two great powers; or any other set of powers for that matter. In the context of Sino-US relations, our leaders have been especially careful not to take sides. This has become a constant refrain, and is illustrated implicitly in the following comments made by the late founding prime minister of Singapore, Lee Kuan Yew, with regard to Sino-US rivalry:

> If the United States attempts to humiliate China, keep it down, it will assure itself an enemy. If instead it accepts China as a big, powerful, rising state and gives it a seat in the boardroom, China will take that place for the foreseeable future. So if I were an American, I would speak well of China, acknowledge it as a great power, applaud its return to its position of respect and restoration of its glorious past, and propose specific, concrete ways to work together. Why should the United States take on China now when it knows that doing so will create an unnecessary adversary for a very long time, and one that will grow in strength and will treat it as an enemy? It is not necessary (cited in Allison and Blackwill, 2013).

Yet it is the very backdrop that we are confronted with today, with all the uncertainties mentioned above, that is compelling us to consider the question that was posed.

It does not help that, if one looks at the latest reporting on developments in Sino-Malaysian and Sino-Philippines relations, these have been cast precisely in this language of (Manila and Kuala Lumpur) choosing between the two powers. Which power are Malaysians and Filipinos portrayed as choosing to align with? According to many media reports, they have all but hopped onto the Chinese bandwagon. The assumptions underlying such accounts however, warrant closer scrutiny. Although it is undeniable that Manila and Kuala Lumpur have deepened bilateral relations with Beijing in recent months, there is no reason why this, on its own, should occasion any suspicion or cause trepidation that the Philippines and Malaysia have gravitated into a Chinese sphere of influence. All countries, including the US, Japan, and even Taiwan, have endeavoured to improve relations with China in recent years. Given the size of the Chinese economy and potential of its consumer market, it would be foolish for any country not to pursue relations with China. At the same time, it would be equally foolhardy to conclude that improving relations with China *ipso facto* means distancing oneself from the US. President Rodrigo Duterte's extensively-covered anti-imperialist rhetorical broadsides notwithstanding, there is little concrete evidence so far that the Philippines is turning its strategic gaze away from the US in any practical sense. Despite President Duterte's threats to end the Philippine alliance with the US, bilateral military exercises between the Philippine and American armed forces continued in 2016, and will do so in 2017 although there are suggestions that these would be reviewed in 2018 (Magan, 2016; Houck, 2016; *The Straits Times*, 2016). Nor are there any indications that Malaysia has in any way downgraded or de-prioritised the US in its foreign policy agenda. At the very least, it is still too early to tell whether decades of *Pax Americana* that have prevailed in the region — especially with regard to security ties between the US and these Southeast Asian countries — is giving way to a *Pax Sinica* for regional states with hitherto close defence ties with the US. On this score, we should bear in mind that although it requires conscious and deliberate effort, the historical record attests to Southeast Asia's ability to balance and engage a range of external powers with different degrees of success, whilst still preserving some measure of autonomy.

THE LIKELIHOOD OF OPEN CONFLICT BETWEEN THE US AND CHINA

Before we consider the scenarios and conditions governing this issue of choice, let us take yet another step back. This notion of choosing sides conjures images of a zero-sum game; one that involves trade-offs; where choosing one side suggests that you are automatically distancing yourself from the other. We have, in a sense, seen this before. During the Cold War, the intense rivalry between the US and the Soviet Union which took place on a global scale, made it exceedingly difficult for smaller states to maintain neutrality or to remain non-aligned, the efforts of the Afro-Asian Movement and Non-Aligned Movement notwithstanding. We live in a different world today, and under present conditions where everything is increasingly inter-dependent, interconnected and digital technology-driven, talk of choosing sides between the US and China represents a false dichotomy, predicated on flawed assumptions. Let me set out my reasons for saying this especially with regard to US-China relations.

First, I believe that Chinese leaders will, in private, grudgingly admit that the US has had a restraining hand on Japan and Taiwan in this region. We have to bear in mind that relations with Japan as well as with Taiwan, are consequential foreign policy issues for the US as far as its policy towards Asia is concerned. It is quite possibly even more so for decision-makers in Beijing. For China, its rivalry with Japan is arguably more complex and acrimonious than its rivalry with the US. As for Taiwan, the Chinese leadership appears to be operating on the assumption that time is on their side when it comes to cross-Strait relations. I am not entirely sure if this is the right way to think about it. As the years pass, efforts to create and strengthen a sense of Taiwanese national identity will surely sink deeper roots, and if this happens, peaceful resolution of cross-Strait relations will be all the more difficult. Given the considerable challenges Beijing faces in dealing with Japan and Taiwan on their own terms, the American contribution to the stability of these sets of relationships by virtue of Washington's restraining influence on Tokyo and Taipei have been and will be instrumental in maintaining relative peace in the region. In other words, even if Beijing is interested to limit the strategic reach of the US in the region, that does not mean that it wants the US to be entirely disengaged from it.

Second, while the Trump presidency might scale back some of its interest and commitment in the region, it is not likely to disengage on its own accord from the region entirely as well. Yes, the halcyon days of the Obama administration's pivot to Asia are gone and will not return any time soon. But "Trumpism" notwithstanding, I think the US not only has much to offer to the region, the former also has much to gain from the latter in terms of economics and security. More importantly, I think that senior cabinet officials as well as Republican Party elders are aware of that, even if President Trump seems nonchalant about it. In point of fact, on the security front, US policy towards the region in the early months of the Trump administration has thrown up more continuity than change with Secretary of Defence James Mattis's assurances to Tokyo and Seoul, and President Trump's reinforcement of these assurances to Prime Minister Shinzo Abe on the occasion of their summit in February 2017.

The economic story, however, might admittedly hold out discomfiting prospects for change. President Trump is clearly intent on rectifying what he and the China hawks in his administration deem to be unfair trade practices on China's part, and they have consequently taken a hard line on China. Underscoring this view is a crucial but implicit assumption: the US has sufficient economic leverage to hurt China more than China can hurt US interests. This is a dangerously misguided assumption.

Let us consider some facts: China is currently the third largest market for US exports, letting in US$104 billion of goods in 2016. Even though this figure has fallen marginally over the last couple of years, with the size of the Chinese market, its increasing affluence and emerging middle class, China will still be a consequential destination for American goods and services. China is also a key node in the global supply chain on which much of US industry relies. While the Trump administration could, in theory, replace Chinese labour with American workers, it is all but certain that this would drive up labour costs for American companies, which in turn could have a negative effect on productivity that has already been on the decline. In other words, the cost of production for US industry will doubtless increase under conditions which President Trump seeks to create, and this cost will ultimately be transferred to the American consumer. Whether President Trump is aware of this or is prepared to admit it, Americans have become avid consumers of Chinese goods. The US is the largest market for Chinese products, which in turn accounts for the sizeable trade deficit between the two countries. While China would obviously be hurt by higher tariffs, raising them will also have a significant impact for consumption patterns of the average American.

In other words, the Trump administration might soon realise that the interests of the American people are better served by more conciliatory methods of rectifying the trade imbalance with China.

Third, following on from the previous point is the fact that China is already an economic powerhouse with growing political influence. This influence will only increase in the coming years with the One Belt One Road initiative and the Asian Infrastructure Investment Bank. So, omitting or eliminating Beijing from the regional equation is simply ludicrous. It is a difficult thing to imagine, and impossible to implement.

Fourth, we need to remember that, rhetoric aside, the scope and depth of bilateral relations between the US and China have widened and deepened considerably over the years. Not too long ago, bilateral relations essentially focused on a small basket of issues: cross-Strait relations, exchange rate of the *renminbi* and bilateral trade. Over the last few years, it has expanded to cover a wider range of issues. Here we are talking about territorial disputes, regional economic trade initiatives and other global issues like climate change, nonproliferation, counterterrorism and cybersecurity. The number of official and unofficial channels for them to discuss these issues have also increased. To that effect, it is notable that Secretary of State Rex Tillerson acknowledged the broad scope of Sino-US relations during his recent visit to Beijing.

So simply put, this bilateral relationship is the most complex relationship between two great powers that the world has ever seen. Their interests intertwine and overlap in ways that makes the prospect of open conflict between them difficult to fathom.

SO WHAT IF WE HAVE TO CHOOSE?

Let us nonetheless think about that scenario of Singapore having to choose sides. What sort of conditions would lead us to such a scenario? In other words, let me contradict all that I have argued earlier and draw out some possible scenarios. Let me discuss five.

First is the election of an unpredictable, impulsive, self-absorbed, vengeful president in the US who would refuse to heed the counsel of others. Needless to say, this is a concern with the current president. However, regardless of the validity of misgivings towards President Trump's character and personality, not to mention his lack of political experience, we have to bear in mind that he has in fact surrounded himself with a very strong national security and foreign policy team. James Mattis, H. R. McMaster and John Kelly are strong and respected leaders with accomplished military credentials. None of them are "yes men". While there are concerns that as secretary of state, Tillerson has yet to demonstrate leadership in what is seen as the most senior cabinet position, few doubt his credentials and professional qualities honed in the private sector. At the same time, there are undeniable reservations about Steve Bannon, Donald Trump's presidential advisor and chief ideologue, as well as the China hawks who populate the trade office and commerce department, including Robert Lighthizer, Wilbur Ross and Peter Navarro.

Second is that of nationalist hawks tightening their grip on power in China. They may be found predominantly but not solely in the People's Liberation Army, and this is the segment of Chinese society that has no reservations when it comes to thinking, talking and planning for conflict with the US. More importantly, they have no patience to suffer the anxieties of small states which may be caught in-between that conflict. They believe that the rise of China is inevitable and that the US and its friends are basically standing in its way.

Third is if there is a serious breakdown in Sino-US relations, which obviously is a scenario that flows from the first and second scenarios. In this case, we are envisaging a situation akin to the Cold War and all those images conjured by the Thucydides Trap, and discussions emerging from that. Even then, as I have written elsewhere, choosing sides under such circumstances is likely to be as costly a decision for a small state like Singapore as standing on the sidelines (Liow, 2017).

Fourth is if an implicit agreement emerges between the US and China to create spheres of influence or rather spheres of predominant interests as it is unlikely either is going to be willing to cede influence in a particular region completely to the other. The South China Sea would be an interesting bellwether of that possibility because it seems unlikely that the US under Trump, or even under Obama at the time, will be prepared to go out of its way to defend the Philippines' interests over a few features that are submerged at high tide.

Fifth is the scenario of a failure of Singapore's diplomacy. For a good part of the post-Vietnam War era, Singapore has worked hard to avoid being put in the sort of situation that is being contemplated here. This being the case, if our leaders find themselves in a position where they have no choice but to choose sides between the two superpowers, it essentially implies that the diplomatic and political elite of the day may well have failed to "hold the line."

CHOOSING SIDES: THE TERMS

Finally, if we did find ourselves in that position of having to choose between alignment with the US or China, the follow-up question would be: On what terms would we make that choice? Let me offer some thoughts on this.

First, if we choose, we must choose on the basis of interests, not countries. It may be a cliché, but it is worth reiterating that we are pro-interests not pro-this or pro-that power. Also, any choice that is made cannot be made at gunpoint (whether literally or figuratively). It has to be an informed choice to secure Singapore's national interests, and it is a choice that would have to be conveyed to the people; their support and endorsement will have to be secured.

Second, if we choose, it must be understood that there should be no interference in domestic politics by that power. In reality, this is likely to be difficult because if we were to capitulate and make concessions, it would be a slippery slope where we would be expected to make even more concessions over time. Keeping that influence and those expectations at bay will be a challenge for the government of the day in Singapore.

Third, we have to be mindful of the perceptions created in our neighbourhood. If making a choice means making concessions, we must be very careful of the signals that are being sent in the process of doing that. Simply put, we may send the wrong signals or other states may read the wrong signals and draw the wrong conclusions from our actions — that Singapore is a pushover. It would not be in our interest to send such a signal, consciously or otherwise. Bear in mind that Singapore is not unfamiliar with bullies.

Fourth, we need to remember that the US and China are not the only major powers of consequence in the region. Again, the question has been cast in that way, but the reality is likely to be considerably more complex. The Sino-US relationship is going to be a key feature of regional affairs in the foreseeable future, but it is not going to be the only determinant of the regional geopolitical landscape. Other powers will also matter, such as Japan, India, Australia and even Russia. Singapore will have to continue deepening our relationships with them too even as we keep one eye constantly trained on developments in Sino-US relations.

Finally, there is ASEAN. It is probably not the best time to talk about ASEAN unity. Indeed, ASEAN has seen better days as far as its unity and cohesion are concerned. Nevertheless, we need to be mindful of the fact that small states in Southeast Asia are facing the same challenge, the same dilemma with regard to the US and China. It is not something that Singapore alone will be confronted with. Other states in the region are pondering how to navigate the waters of great power politics. I think it would be very useful for Singapore to not just look at the situation from purely the point of view of what Singapore's interests are, but also in relation to, and in cohesion with our neighbours who are facing similar challenges. However weak ASEAN may be, there is still strength in numbers, and this strength will afford us some much-needed autonomy from the centrifugal forces of great power politics, provided ASEAN can indeed remain united.

REFERENCES

Allison, G., & Blackwill, R. (2013, March 5). Interview: Lee Kuan Yew on the future of US-China relations. *The Atlantic.* Retrieved from: https://www.theatlantic.com/china/archive/2013/03/interview-lee-kuan-yew-on-the-future-of-us-china-relations/273657/.

Houck, C. (2016, November 15). US troops are still in the Philippines, despite Duterte's insults and threats. *Defence One.* Retrieved from: http://www.defenseone.com/news/2016/11/us-troops-are-still-philippinesregardless-what-duterte-says/133195/.

Magan, G. (2016, October 4). Philippines, US joint military exercises despite Duterte's comments. *Philippine News.* Retrieved from: https://philnews.ph/2016/10/04/Philippines-us-hold-joint-military-exercises-despite-dutertes-comments/.

Liow, J. C. (2017, January 22). Trump's ascent should prompt Southeast Asia to look back. *Nikkei Asian Review.* Retrieved from: https://asia.nikkei.com/Viewpoints/Joseph-Chinyong-Liow/Trump-s-ascent-should-prompt-Southeast-Asia-to-look-back.

The Straits Times. (2016, September 29). Philippines says joint military exercise with US to go ahead in 2017, but will review 2018 drills. Retrieved from: http://www.straitstimes.com/asia/se-asia/philippines-say-will-go-ahead-with-joint-military-exercise-with-us-in-2017-but.

17

What if Singapore Becomes a Two- or Multi-Party System?

ONG YE KUNG

"What if Singapore becomes a two- or multi-party system?"

I could make this a boring discussion by insisting that we are already a multi-party system since many parties participate in our general elections, but that would be a cop out.

Instead, let us train our attention on the elephant in the room — which is the People's Action Party (PAP). The scenario painted for us is that by 2065, it is replaced by several smaller elephants — political parties — that will take turns to govern after each election or rule through coalitions.

This will be a drastic departure from the status quo which we cannot rule out half a century from now. The question is: What happens then?

I would like to present my thoughts in three parts. First, while life will change in many ways, we will adapt and in many ways, life will go on. Second, I will explain why this can give rise to a couple of serious long-term risks for Singapore. Third, I will address the question that many Singaporeans will also ask: "What is the PAP going to do about it?"

LIFE GOES ON

First, what will change and yet, how will life go on?

A major change that will stem from becoming a multi-party system will be the shifting of the political ground. Expect intense jostling — different parties reaching out to various groups to garner support. The trade union movement may not be as cohesive as it is today where it works with the PAP in a symbiotic relationship. It may be split into two or more groupings, or there may be a competing federation, like in 1961 when the existing Singapore Trades Union Congress split into the Singapore Association of Trade Unions and the National Trades Union Congress. Likewise, there will be split affiliations amongst associations, clans, societies, recreational clubs, civil society organisations, socio-political sites, sports and arts bodies, and so on. Media houses may split too.

It is not a new phenomenon. We have seen this happen in more hotly contested constituencies. After the general election in 2011 when the Workers' Party (WP) won Aljunied Group Representation Constituency (GRC), I found myself becoming the opposition politician in that GRC. There were groups that would invite me as guest-of-honour to their events, and others that would invite the WP members of parliament. Most would invite both, and I got the feeling that the guests enjoyed watching the jostling. In a multi-party system, the scale of that happening will likely be larger, nationwide, at events, and behind the scenes.

I believe the institution that is most likely to be tested is the civil service. The holy grail of the civil service is to be politically neutral and serve which-ever party forms the government regardless of how different the incoming party may be from the outgoing one in governance philosophy. Public service officers must lay out the policy options, state the pros and cons, let the political leaders with the mandate decide, and then, they must support the decision. It is a professional ideal, but in practice, it is easier said than done. You can work on one set of policies for five years and someone new can come along to ask you to undo everything you have done and move in a new direction. We see that happening now — the Affordable Healthcare Act in the United States (US) is being unwound, the country has also withdrawn from the Trans-Pacific Partnership. That can be very frustrating and dis-heartening to public service leaders.

It is useful to see how other countries deal with it. America ended up politicising the higher echelons of its civil service. The top few layers of bureaucrats are political appointees, and whenever there is a change in who is the president, they are all replaced. That is why the new Trump adminis-tration has to make 4,000 appointments.

The alternative is the Australian or the British system, where all civil servants in the ministries stay intact, but a minister's office is packed with his own staffers — presumably more aligned to his thinking. In Australia, ministers spend most of their time with these staffers in parliament, and not the civil servants in the ministries — because parliament is where the political contest is.

We will have to adapt to all these if the scenario comes to pass, which also means that the status quo as we know it will change. But adapt we will.

THE MAJOR RISKS

Second, I will touch on the real long-term risks for Singapore of a multi-party system that are beyond adapting and getting used to. The risk is not so much a result of being in a multi-party system per se, but the forces and processes that will lead us there.

For a two- or multi-party system to take shape, there must first have been at least two paths, sufficiently different, for our country to take. These paths can be a narrow fork in the road that can even merge further down, or a T-junction pointing in opposite directions and will never meet.

Take the United Kingdom (UK) for example. From the mid-1990s to early 2010s, the Conservatives and New Labour both believed in a pro-business, market economy that upholds equality of opportunities instead of equality in outcomes. Both eschewed labour unrest and strikes — which was a major shift for New Labour. The key divergence in policy was probably in their attitudes towards the European Union (EU). Today, that has widened into a gulf between those who believe in the idea of the UK leaving the EU or "Brexit" in one camp and that of remaining in the EU, in the other camp. That difference has split British society between the young and old, urban and rural residents, the more and the less educated.

In the US, the key historical divergence between the Republicans and Democrats was slavery. The situation has evolved. Slavery is no more, and today, the two parties hold distinct views on the size of government, taxation, abortion and gun control. In the 2016 presidential election, those positions widened, pitting nationalism against globalisation, whites versus people of other races. Both presidential candidates have openly acknowledged that it was a bitter and divisive election.

Political parties are essential in representing the diverse views of people, and elections, a necessary and relatively peaceful process by which to find compromises in policy positions to seek a way forward for the country. This is the essence of democracy. Yet, that same defining quality can take a nasty twist, sow discord and divide societies. Hence Winston Churchill said, "… democracy is the worst form of Government except all those other forms that have been tried from time to time."

Fifty years from now, if we have a multi-party system, what will define the key political differences between political parties? Where will that partisan line emerge? Would it be over the extent to which we should subsidise public services, healthcare and social assistance? If that is so, it may well be something we can manage. What if it is over something more sinister that divides Singapore by race, language or religion? As we all know, politics, race and religion is a toxic mix. If that happens, we will be broken as a country and society.

Another major risk is whether a multi-party system will slow down decision-making and our nimbleness in navigating an ever-changing external environment. If we had a multi-party system back in 1965, would we have become a developed economy and country so quickly?

Back then, in that post-colonial era, we could move to attract foreign direct investment from multinational corporations when it was not politically correct to do so. We forged omni-directional, bilateral free trade agreements while others pledged allegiance to the World Trade Organization's multilateral system. We must move fast in embracing new digital technologies, even though it can be uncomfortable and disruptive.

If we envisage a future of tough challenges — a shifting geopolitical landscape, more intense economic competition, worrying demographic trends, rising sea levels — unity, common purpose and the ability to move faster than others will be central and vital for us. While other countries are either slow but big, or small but fast, will we end up suffering the worst of both worlds — small and slow?

The current system has worked well for the majority of Singaporeans so far. It still gets my vote as the best system for Singapore.

HERE'S WHAT WE NEED TO DO

So, given these risks, what can the PAP do about them?

To answer this question, let me rewind to 2011 when I was first introduced as a PAP candidate. I was asked by a journalist what I thought of a single-party system in Singapore. I said that our equilibrium as a small country may well be single-party rule. That party can be the PAP today, but some other party in the future — so long it is the most capable at that time.

You know that between Singaporeans living in Changi and Jurong, their concerns and views on national issues may be somewhat different, but nothing compared to the great differences you are likely to find between people living in Alaska and New York City, Jakarta and the eastern- and western-most places in the Indonesian archipelago. For big countries, geographical separation translates into different lifestyles, outlook, values and political affinities, which then lends itself to multi-party politics.

The one-party dominant system in the case of Singapore, is not a prescription, but the most likely outcome of choice — a result of free and fair elections. It is no different from Massachusetts being dominated by Democrats for long periods, or Scotland dominated by Labour previously, and now, the Scottish National Party. Smallness and concentration do often come together.

So the answer to the question of what the PAP is going to do about it is that we must make sure the current system continues to work for all Singaporeans!

To do so, we must understand what factors made it work so far. Complacency, elitism and corruption are not inevitable outcomes of one-party dominant rule alone. After all, these ills have shown up across all political systems.

The PAP knows that our integrity must be unquestionable. If something goes wrong, it will be rectified and the perpetrators must face the consequences; that action has to be swift.

The PAP must be a party that is open-minded. It has to keep up with the changing expectations of the population — so that we can be at the forefront of new ideas, with policies that are adapted to the changing needs of society and our people. We must never think that today's solutions are the best there are. We have to keep our eyes and ears open to changes in our surroundings, consult widely, improve our co-creation skills, and work together with citizens in finding solutions to unfolding issues. The PAP must attract talent from as diverse a background as possible to serve the country. That is why at the end of every parliamentary term, the PAP replaces a quarter to a third of the people we place on our electoral slates compared to the previous one.

The PAP must constantly reflect on its performance especially in areas that it has not done well, and even on why the Singapore Dream may not have worked out so well for some Singaporeans. Our policies must be rooted in the ground; a sizeable proportion of our work must be on the ground. In this age of inequality, ours cannot just be a system which rewards only the best and brightest. It must also be a system that compensates for poor family circumstances and the role of luck.

CONCLUSION

Every country in the world is different. A country's success is idiosyncratic and can never be replicated wholesale by another. The formula for success is based on different political processes. Singapore's formula may well be a single-party system.

Ultimately, the political future of a country will be determined by the will of its people. If the people wish for a change to a multi-party system, it will be so. The job of the opposition parties is to highlight to people the risks of the current system. Likewise, it is the job of the PAP today to do our best to make sure that Singapore flourishes, point out the risks of a multi-party system for a small country like ours and keep out the ills of complacency, elitism and corruption.

Whatever the "what ifs" — single- or multi-party system — among all parties and all Singaporeans, we need singularity of purpose and a wide agreement on the means of implementing this purpose. This is not mere politics, but it is about our collective journey, as a people, as a country, to improve the lives of all.

18

The Real Question Behind "What if Singapore Becomes a Two- or Multi-Party System?"

HO KWON PING

THE REAL QUESTION: WHAT IF THE PAP'S POLITICAL DOMINANCE IS BROKEN

After Donald Trump's almost surreal inauguration on January 20, 2017, the Institute of Policy Studies' (IPS) conference entitled "What If" appears not just prescient in hindsight, but is an urgently needed exercise in future-think. The unthinkable can become the improbable, then the quite possible and sometimes, even reality in an increasingly uncertain world.

So, what is the unthinkable, improbable, what-if political scenario for Singapore?

Here, IPS is being coy with its disingenuously bland topic: "What if Singapore becomes a two- or multi-party system?" After all, unless IPS believes Singapore is like Cuba or North Korea, it is quite obvious that we are *already* a multi-party system to the extent that multiple parties freely and openly contend in general elections. However, as a *one-party dominant* system, we do not have a *pendulum* democracy where a dynamic political equilibrium is sustained over the long term through political power alternating between two dominant parties providing checks and balances against each other.

IPS' real question is what in my recent book *The Ocean in a Drop* I called the elephant-in-the-room issue: What if one-party dominance is broken, the People's Action Party (PAP) loses in a general election and another political party forms the government?

The PAP itself considered this possibility long ago. Many will recall that the pioneer PAP prime minister, the late Mr Lee Kuan Yew, foresaw that scenario of a "freak election" where an electorate may (in his view) unintentionally and irresponsibly vote out the PAP. His solution was to create the Elected Presidency as a check against what he considered a "rogue government".

What if, however, a freak election is not a freak event but instead becomes institutionalised and Singapore does become a pendulum democracy? Would it be good, bad, or neutral for Singaporeans? How likely is it?

A traditional liberal would welcome this prospect as a sign of progress towards full participatory democracy. After all, one of the touchstones of Western liberal democracy is the concept of a two-party pendulum democracy as the bulwark of long-term, sustainable governance. After Brexit, Donald Trump and other recent or upcoming elections in Europe, we know that faith in traditional Western liberal democracy has been shaken enough for it to no longer be the yardstick by which political maturity or sustainability is measured. This is especially among those who are alarmed by the populist, nationalist sentiments that seemed to have carried the ground in the Brexit Referendum and American election; one where the narrative was to exclude or marginalise minorities and foreigners, and stoke ambivalence against globalisation. It seemed like democracy had turned in on itself with those illiberal choices.

A more universal and comprehensive yardstick is the quality of the social contract between a political leadership and its body politic regardless of whether the formal political structure is a two-party pendulum democracy, a monopolistic Communist regime, or a single-party dominant system. The depth of that social contract and by implication, the political legitimacy of the ruling elite, depends on a complex and yet subtle blend of factors for which successive Chinese dynasties coined the euphemism, "the mandate of heaven".

Should that mandate ever erode beyond repair, no amount of two-party or multi-party democracy can save a political regime or ruling dynasty. Traditional pendulum politics does not by itself guarantee genuine participatory democracy: the present crisis of liberal democracy and lurch towards extremism and populism in the United States and Europe, as mentioned above, is eloquent testimony to this depressing reality.

THE REAL CONCERN BEHIND ANTICIPATING POLITICAL CHANGE IN SINGAPORE

Against this backdrop then, the critical question facing Singapore in 2065 is not simply whether an accidental freak election or a sustainable pendulum democracy should or might occur. It is about whether the social contract between elite governance and the body politic can become so strained and frayed that a crisis of political legitimacy may thrust unexpected, extremist scenarios ranging from rule by a military-dominated junta to unstable coalition governments, into reality.

In other words, what might happen to get us from where we are today, a bastion of political stability, to the uncertainties now plaguing the rest of the world? Let me ask and then answer three further questions in pursuit of this issue.

First, what events could lead to a massive loss of legitimacy or confidence in the PAP or the current political system?

Second, what are the chances of these events happening?

Third, is a two-party pendulum democracy a likely, stable and sustainable option? Alternatively, what might realistically evolve in the specific Singapore context?

Let me address the first question in a circumspect manner, by alluding to other Asian democracies. The closest though imperfect parallels are India and Taiwan. In both countries, the founding party of the nation — the Indian Congress party and the Kuomintang (KMT) — were led by charismatic leaders, Jawaharlal Nehru and Chiang Kai Shek, respectively. They were worlds apart both in personality as well as in their party structures but possessed as founding fathers, an unquestioned legitimacy. After their passing, their offspring — Indira Gandhi and Chiang Ching Kuo — succeeded them (albeit with brief interludes in India) but after them, both the party leadership and parties themselves started to decline.

Three identical things happened in both parties:

First, nepotism prevented the rise of younger, meritocratic elites vying within the party for ascendancy, resulting in sycophants all clustering around the dynastic heirs like in some archaic monarchy.

Second, the values, policies and solutions which led the founding party to success became sacrosanct; sacred cows that could not be questioned even if their relevance started to wane. A sense of political complacency settled like fine dust over even the internal insurgents and overcame any impetus towards change.

Third, a culture of entitlement led to endemic corruption, both political and financial, the final blow in an inexorable decline of legitimacy.

Should that fate, which has befallen almost all founding parties in electoral democracies over time affect the PAP in coming decades, we have the scenario for disruptive change.

The second question is: how likely is this to happen?

The short answer is: not very likely in the next quarter-century, or around 20 to 25 years. Beyond that, no one knows.

Why 20 years — perhaps too optimistic for some and too pessimistic for others? I chose this time span because I assume that under our present system, even when the present prime minister, Mr Lee Hsien Loong retires, he will assume the mantle of senior minister or minister mentor, and his cohort of leaders will remain like tribal elders — there to guide successive leadership teams not so much in policymaking but in the preservation of political values, self-discipline and vision which congeal into a lasting political culture.

History has shown that the values of a founding political culture can usually be transmitted with vigour down three to four generations. Beyond that, complacency and entitlement usually overwhelm the messianic urgency and self-discipline found in pioneer values. One can only hope that future PAP leaders after our current leadership have long passed from the scene, can learn from history.

They will have a few advantages, not least being a young nation, a new political culture of anti-corruption, meritocracy and multiculturalism did not have to battle the centuries of deep divisions which afflicted say, Indian civilisation. As Sri Lanka's civil war has shown, a relatively short period of self-serving political opportunism and populism can spiral out of control rapidly. So who is to say, from what we have already seen with the descent into opportunism in even mature, developed European and American societies, that our future leaders will be so self-disciplined as to eschew even a shred of self-interest, especially if their popularity starts to wane?

As for nepotism, there are no current signs of this happening with a Lee dynasty clinging to power or promoting only its relatives. Anti-corruption has now become not just government policy but a fundamental value of our people. The government has shown signs that even sacred cow policies can be re-examined if they are no longer relevant. We witnessed the PAP government accept the need to tighten up the economy's reliance on cheaper foreign manpower in 2010; reverse its stance on ministerial salaries and slash them by more than a third in 2012; reduce the over-emphasis on academic credentials with the calibration of how the high-stakes Primary School Leaving Examinations are graded as announced in 2013; and then, place more emphasis on skills-training, competencies, performance and there-fore give recognition to a "continuous meritocracy" in hiring and rewarding workers, starting with changes in public service personnel policies, announced in 2014. We can think of more.

For those reasons, I remain, using that clichéd phrase, cautiously optimistic. We know however that to some extent, that is whistling in the dark.

When I was a student in Taiwan in the late 1960s, no one could have imagined the decline of the KMT and its future electoral loss, or the rise of a seemingly radical party like the Democratic Progressive Party. It all happened in a few decades. It can happen here too.

The third and possibly most intriguing question is whether the scenario leading towards pendulum democracy in Singapore is the most desirable and likely long-term outcome? And if not, what are the alternatives?

Here we have a conundrum. History has generally shown, despite recent events in the West, that a pendulum democracy offers a more sustainable, dynamic equilibrium than a single-party dominant system which has no competition and falls into complacent entitlement.

On the other hand, to move from the generally well-governed stability of our current single-party dominant system to a pendulum democracy implies that a massive loss of legitimacy by the ruling party has to first occur. That is not necessarily desirable, and of course, not even likely given the current robustness of the PAP and the weakness of the opposition parties.

DODGING POLITICAL OSSIFICATION AND A FRAYING
SOCIAL COMPACT — TWO SUGGESTIONS

The danger of a single-party dominant system is political ossification over time, as the sense of entitlement encourages the nepotism, complacency and corruption which inevitably led to the demise — and eventual re-emergence of course — of even the most idealistic founding parties, some of which I have mentioned above.

Therefore one viable alternative is to institutionalise internal policy competition and deepen internal democracy within the PAP, beyond just secret elections to a central committee or politburo.

Several very different and dominant Asian political parties — from those in Japan to China to Vietnam — already have intra-party competition through competing internal factions and cliques, overseen and endorsed by an informal cabal of elders. It can produce a reasonably sustainable succession process where competition allows the most capable and broadly popular leaders to emerge.

However, because this is largely informal, it is subject to back-room intrigue and horse-trading to the benefit of influential king-makers. It is also a competition over individuals, and not a competition of ideas.

An attempt to institutionalise a transparent internal competitive selection process not just for leadership roles but between party caucuses which represent different philosophical or policy tendencies, may be an innovative and sustainable way to combat complacency in long-ruling founding parties.

By itself however, internal party competition cannot ensure that a political elite will remain relevant to the needs of a changing population. On the contrary, civil society must be further empowered as a partner to strengthen the social contract, and also act as a check against inept or corrupt governance.

This involves nourishing civil society players with that lifeblood of robust discussion: freely available and largely unrestricted information. It is something I advocated in my final IPS-Nathan lecture, and I notice that we are steadily improving on that front. The government's statistics department is making more data available on its website as well as on the more interactive platform, data.gov.sg modelled on the American open data site, and when any points of controversy in public policy emerge, you can be sure you will find some issue-specific data on the site called "factually". The notion that the less information the public has equates to the less they can criticise, is a natural, universal, bureaucratic impulse which is slowly giving way to the realisation that wide and deep access to information is a key measure of participatory democracy.

Access to information enables the public to robustly debate and articulate ground-up responses to the pressing societal issues of the day. An information-rich society is all the more important since we have seen in the recent US presidential election, how social media can easily distort facts and even manufacture dis-information.

Our government was prescient to warn about the inherent flaws and anti-democratic dangers of unfettered social media, but the preservation of a social contract that might begin to fray cannot be achieved by an instinctive knee-jerk clampdown on social media, even if it were possible in the digital age.

The solution is not in more regulation and censorship, but in more citizen watchdogs monitoring falsehoods and pointing these out. Lies can only be destroyed by the sunlight of diverse and plentiful sources of the truth, and by civil society constantly building up its intellectual sinews to grapple with the arguments about current approaches in public policy and governance, as well as options for future.

In conclusion, 2065 is a destination for which the journey is fraught with uncertainties. The simplistic solution which traditional liberal democrats have held out — a pendulum form of democracy — is not necessarily the most desirable or the most likely scenario for Singapore. Yet the track record of continuously ruling founding parties has not been good. How the PAP can reinvent itself with the benefit of historical hindsight to ensure robust internal competition, and also truly engage civil society in genuine participatory democracy, will shape the future of our nation.

CHAPTER 19

Strategic Planning for Singapore's Future

HENG SWEE KEAT

The budget is a strategic plan for Singapore. The budget cannot just be about taxes, revenue and expenditure. Why are we collecting revenue? What for and where are we spending it? Why are we spending it? Are we planning for the long haul? Are we planning for a better Singapore? I think those are the important questions. These are the issue that I think we ought to concentrate on. It is not just what the budget can do or what government can do but what all of us in Singapore can do together.

Let me start with a preview of the budget. First, government spending has more than doubled in the last decade from S$33 billion in the financial year 2007 to S$71 billion in the financial year 2016. This is a very high rate of increase. So, the question is where has the money gone to? If you just concentrate on social spending, it has gone up from 35 per cent of S$33 billion in 2007 to 40 per cent of S$71 billion in 2017.

The Ministry of Education (MOE) accounted for 22.8 per cent of the pie in 2007. In 2016, it was 17.7 per cent. So, are we spending less on education? No, because the whole pie has grown. We are spending more on education despite the fact that we are having falling enrolments and we are closing schools. Yet, we are spending more. We are spending more per child and per individual. This is partly because we are spending more in our schools and in the Institutes of Higher Learning (IHLs) and because we have extended programmes like SkillsFuture and other lifelong learning programmes. That is the part of our social budget.

The Ministry of Health (MOH) accounted for 6.7 per cent of S$33 billion, and last year, it more than doubled to 13.7 per cent of a much, much bigger base of S$71 billion. The Ministry of Social and Family Development (MSF) expenditures accounted for 3.5 per cent of the total expenditure. The Ministry of Culture, Community and Youth (MCCY) accounted for 3 per cent and a segment of manpower expenditures dealing with workers like worker upgrading has gone up as well. So, our social spending has gone up significantly.

While the overall percentage of security spending has come down, the absolute number has continued to go up. In terms of infrastructure and transport, the one very interesting set of numbers is from the Ministry of Transport (MOT). MOT accounted for 5.9 per cent of the budget in 2007 and it has gone up to 14.6 per cent in 2016. So, again it has more than doubled. Why? It is not only the spending on infrastructure like rail lines and maintenance work, but also the new bus services, the bus services plan and very significant changes within just ten years.

Now, where did the money come from? The one data point which I hope that everyone here can bear in mind is that back in 2007, the contribution from the reserves was 5.6 per cent and in 2016, the contribution from the reserves was 17.3 per cent. Of all revenue sources, it is the single largest contribution category today — more than corporate income tax, GST or personal income tax. To put it another way, if we had not used contributions from reserves, your personal income tax, GST or corporate income tax could have doubled. All of these are not terribly great solutions. So, I know that many of you, as shown in the survey, think that we should be spending more reserves and it is a subject which we can discuss in detail. For now, I thought that we must have some perspective on where the money is coming from.

Let me move on to three new topics. I will talk about three issues to set the stage for further discussion. Firstly, we are undergoing a major demographic transition. This major demographic transition would have implications on many of the issues that you and I and every Singaporean, everyone living in Singapore, is concerned with. Whether it is an issue relating to healthcare, financial adequacy, mobility, transport, jobs or the future economy, each and every one of these issues is a very big topic by itself. I think we ought to drill deep into each of these issues to understand what it all means.

For instance, in healthcare, how would the demand pattern change in the coming years as our population goes through that demographic transition? What sort of illness will be more prevalent and how would that manifest itself? On the supply side, do we have enough doctors, healthcare workers and healthcare professionals to manage the transition? Do we have enough of the right expertise? Where is the care best done? Is it in the acute hospital or in the community hospital? Is it in a community? Is it at home? For each of these, what are the pros and cons? How do we go about deciding on what is the best system? It is not just looking at it from the point of view of an acute hospital versus a community hospital. We should look at it as totality and ask what the best way of dealing with it is. What is the best way of managing it so that we can be successful? The same applies to education, defence and security. Our changing demographic pattern will have a significant impact on each of these single item issues. For example, what does changing demography mean for the economy? It is going to be a significant set of changes. My first point is that each issue requires very useful and deep discussion.

Secondly, beyond a single issue, we really must think of these issues together. How would issue A interact with issue B? How would healthcare interact with the economy, jobs and social care? If we were to take a segmented approach and say this is issue A, this is issue B and this is issue C, and we tackle each one separately, I think we are going to be lost. This is because we might be working across purpose and the outcome may not be as good as if we work together. When I was in MOE, and even now in MOF, I saw the large number of cross-disciplinary, interdisciplinary study centres, policy think tanks and so on, across all universities in the world. This is a new growth industry. If studying an issue requires so much work and cross-disciplinary effort, how much more do we need to do if we are going to do something about an issue? The policy work and the actual work related to an issue will be far better dealt with by a cross-disciplinary approach. Therefore, for many of these issues, we need to take that view.

Let me just give you two illustrations of what I mean. One is the interaction between work, health and financial security. I think many of you are aware that Japan is also facing a very rapidly ageing population. In Japan, they found that the older workers who continued working, regardless of whether they needed the income or not, were healthier. This is because work provides a platform for social interaction which staying at home just does not provide. So, we cannot be thinking about work in isolation from health and financial security.

The second example has got to do with our own experience with health and social care. When we first started the Pioneer Generation Package (PGP), we were quite concerned as to whether our pioneer generation would understand the intricacies of the scheme. We then appointed pioneer generation ambassadors — neighbours staying in the vicinity — who would go out and explain this package to our pioneer generation. Interestingly, there were many who raised issues which were not about healthcare. There were issues relating to finance, their family members, staying alone and loneliness and needing other sources of care. For every one of those issues, there is an agency, ministry or people responsible, but there is clearly a gap at the frontline. There is a gap in terms of how well we are delivering that service to the seniors who need it. So, we piloted the idea of "pioneer generation ambassadors" and achieved some good outcomes.

At the last budget, I had a very good discussion with Minister Gan Kim Yong and we decided that we will look at a community network of seniors. The community network of seniors also comprised neighbours staying in the vicinity and neighbourhood who would explain to the seniors in their area about some of the activities around them and asked them what their needs were. They have come up with very interesting results. We were able to meet a very important and growing need in our society. We need to look at the issues in a much more cross-disciplinary way and across agencies and ministries. Just some weeks back, I had a very interesting discussion with Minister Gan Kim Yong, Minister Grace Fu, Minister Desmond Lee and Speaker Tan Chuan-Jin because all of them are very concerned about the issues of seniors. We had an excellent discussion on what we need to do differently in the coming years.

A few days back, I read in *The Straits Times* and in the *New York Times International Edition* that the UK has appointed a Minister of Loneliness. Now, I must say that the UK must be the first country in the world to appoint a Minister of Loneliness. A report from the Joe Cox Commission found that nine million people are either often or are always feeling lonely. The sense of loneliness actually affects all age groups but it affects the elderly even more. Majority of those who are 75 and above live alone. I notice that as well in my own work in the constituency. Now, interestingly, after the report came out, the UK was the first to act.

It is not alone. The former Surgeon General of the US then estimated that in the US, 40 per cent suffer from loneliness of some form. Being a former Surgeon General, he talked about how that is a health epidemic. So, it is very important for us not to look at issues in isolation. I am really very glad that my colleagues in the Ministries are dealing with this. Ministers Kim Yong, Grace, Desmond and Speaker Chuan-Jin have been very concerned and have been working together on this. We started this work a lot earlier, and in fact, Minister Gan Kim Yong and Minister Desmond Lee co-chaired a Committee on Ageing. They have been doing a lot of work. So, we are actually not starting from scratch, we are starting from a position of strength and I hope that we can do more. I will be happy to hear your views on what we can do on this front.

My third point concerns the implications of this change on Singapore and ageing as a global phenomenon. We are not the only society that is ageing rapidly, many other societies are and what are the implications? There are pluses and minuses. The plus is that we can now work with many more countries to see how we can tackle common challenges, in particular in the area of healthcare. Solutions that are tried in one place could probably be useful to Singapore and so on. Hopefully, the global budget for doing research in this area will increase and we can all do it together.

The minus is this: we do not know how ageing will affect other societies. In fact, we cannot even be sure how ageing will affect our own society. What is the impact on the psychology of our people? Do our people become more withdrawn as we have seen in some societies? Will there be a withdrawal from the global system? Globalisation is not something to be taken for granted because if the stresses and strains are great, partly because of ageing and the inability of older workers to train, retrain and learn new things, you can expect that many other societies would think about protecting themselves first. They will first make their own society great again before thinking about the impact on others. What is the impact on us in that scenario? Now, fortunately, I must say that it is to the great credit of former Minister George Yeo, who started the wave of Free Trade Agreement almost 20 years ago, that we now have a whole range of free trade agreements. It provides a bit of insulation, but is not something to be taken for granted. The global order can change very quickly. I do not think anybody would have expected that America would withdraw from the Trans-Pacific Partnership (TPP) just like that, but it happened. Let us be very careful about what is happening globally.

Of the other two global forces that are going to have a significant impact on us, the first is advances in technology. The Germans talk about Industry 4.0, and there is a very lively debate on this whole issue of how information and communication technology (ICT) will affect even the traditional manufacturing industry. The impact of ICT and of technology in general on many industries will not be easy to predict. What is the impact of genomics on healthcare? What is the impact of genomics and ICT, together, on healthcare? A whole new range of issues have been thrown up, not just the social and ethical issue, but also very important economic issues. While we talk about our ageing population and how we need to prepare our older workers better for changes, we have to bear in mind that our education system was not as good as it is today when we first became independent. In fact, many of my classmates in my primary school did not make it past the Primary School Leaving Examinations (PSLE) and they started work when they were very young. Retraining some of these older workers today is going to be quite difficult.

So, fortunately, I think our education system has improved a great deal but when we talk about the future of work, industry and technology, we have to take a concerted effort to think about how we can redesign jobs. We may need to think about how to extend the retirement age, and for that matter, rethink the whole concept of retirement. Why should people retire? Even as we do that, we should be very careful that we do not deprive the young people of opportunities. What is the balance we need to create in our society to manage that? It is not a simple issue but an issue which we ought to grapple with early. The technological changes throughout the global economy will affect each and every one of us regardless of our age and it will affect our elder workers even more.

I just saw some of the initiatives that have been tried out in Japan. There, they are looking at the use of robots to enable older workers to continue to do fairly difficult manual jobs because the robot takes over the hard work of lifting heavy boxes which enables the elder person to continue working. I went to factories in Singapore recently and looked at how they redesigned jobs to enable this lady, who is now in her late 50s, to continue working in that company. I was really very impressed. So, I asked the management. I said, "Did you do this deliberately or did it happen as an afterthought?" They said, "No, we are very conscious that we must use technology because otherwise we will be displaced as a company. At the same time we also want to create opportunities for the workers who have been with us for so many years so loyally, and therefore, we make a special effort to redesign jobs." I said, "Well, you are a very global company. What are you doing elsewhere?" They are indeed doing something similar elsewhere. My respect for this company went up a few notches. I was really happy that we have such a company in Singapore. So, that is about the future of how you will interact with technology.

Now, the other final global force that I want to talk about is the shifting economic fortunes. This graph, from McKinsey Global Institute, shows an approximation of centres of gravity of the global economy from AD1 to today. Essentially, in the earlier part, Asia was the centre of many economic activities for many years. China and India were agricultural economies and had mastered agriculture. They were the most successful countries in growing their population and their economy. But gradually, it shifted to England as it was England which started the Industrial Revolution. The Industrial Revolution spread to the rest of Europe and then, thereafter, moved over to America. And the centre of gravity of the global economy moved westwards to the US. Then gradually, as the Asian economies re-joined the global economy, given their weight, the centre of gravity started shifting back. And there are some projections that over the next five years or ten years, the centre of gravity will continue moving to this part of the world.

Now, this is going to happen at a time when many economies in Asia are also ageing. What would be the impact of an ageing economy as well as a growing and technologically more advanced global economy for all of us here? I do not think I have the full answer. I have seen many reports speculating on the future of jobs, industry and fortunes. I am not prepared to bet that it will be one way or the other, but I am prepared to bet that it will be different. The more alert we are to this, the better it is.

To sum up, I would say that when we think about the ageing issue, it is important that we do not look at it as a single issue. Neither should we look at it from an agency-centric point of view. It is important for us within Singapore to work across, not just within government agencies, but with the people and private sector. What is it that a private sector should do differently — in the way they think about the economy, jobs and their role in providing some of the support? What is the role of our Voluntary Welfare Organisations (VWO)? What is it that we can do in our own neighbourhoods? What is it that you and I can do together?

What we are seeing is not a single change but really a series of changes happening across space and time. How are these changes going to interact with one another? We cannot predict with accuracy, so what is the best way of dealing with it? I think we can be sure that the rate of change will be faster not just for us but for everyone else around the world. It means that it can be more unsettling and it is all the more critical that we stay together to tackle these changes. If we can put our minds and hearts together, I think we can do a lot more. So, yes, the population is ageing but we can be an ageless society.